Dear Leader...

A PERSONAL GUIDE FOR LEADERS THROUGH PEACE, PANDEMIC AND PROTEST

T.R. Parker

Dedication

This book is dedicated to my parents Bryce and Gloria, who first taught me the meaning of honor, integrity, and leadership with love. To my beloved husband Jorge, for always believing in and supporting me. To my children Khai, Kanai, and Landon, bonus daughter Mimi, and Legacy child Kailand for inspiring me to create a legacy worthy of them.

Special thanks to Tiisetso, Lena and Koko for literally praying me through this process. And finally to all the friends that supported me and cheered me on and to the leaders that strive to be and are the change in this world.

Preface

Dear Leader is a divinely inspired series of thoughts and words birthed from the real-life struggles of myself and leaders I've coached, encountered, or witnessed through my work in leadership. Though this is not a religious book per se, I speak from my own deeply spiritual perspective without requiring the reader to share my beliefs or be of any particular religious sect. I write with the hope that it will lead to great personal introspection, whatever your beliefs. I've chosen to write this work as a series of letters so that leaders who are just starting out, to those ready to retire will be able to read and feel an intimate and personal connection to the experiences as a leader. These letters were written over an extended period of time in response to different experiences - lived and witnessed, and thus are a collection of unique versions of my voice. In the midst of creating this book, the world changed. The Pandemic happened and I felt an added urgency for leaders to hear the perspectives in these pages. This is not a perfect work, it is an intimate and personal one. My desire for sharing these letters is to expand the depth of compassion and outlook of hope for the reader and to showcase different perspectives of leadership that may often be overlooked or omitted when discussing leadership roles.

There are probably a million how-to books and programs on leadership. Many focus on the ABC's and 123's of being a good leader. How to lead with courage. How to make friends while leading; how-to, how-to, how-to! All very good for pumping us up and giving us a strategic blueprint for entering the realm of leadership. However, I am not interested in a simple "How-to", I want to engage you, the reader, by sharing the in's and outs, the up and downs, the good, the bad, and the ugly of wearing the crown of a leader. The struggles behind the glory, the challenges beyond the triumphs. The parts people seldom like to talk about, yet are an intricate part of the journey of any leader. This is not a book of answers, but rather a book of introspection and necessary conversations, mainly with yourself.

Who am I? For most of my life, I've viewed myself as a reluctant leader - one with innate leadership abilities, but with very little interest or willingness to engage them. The firstborn of five, I was often in the "boss'" seat from a very young age. From early on in my life, being responsible was a requirement of my existence. I wasn't in an abusive home. I was simply first-born; an only girl with four brothers. You can imagine the daily requirements to help maintain order in a house full of boys. My parents were entrepreneurs who ran a thriving business from our home and this required that I take on certain responsibilities to help in the household. That was my introduction to leadership.

I began answering phones in our family business as early as 10 years old. When I wasn't assisting in the family business, the family was my business. I was in charge of cleaning, maintaining, and organizing my brothers and the house while my parents met with clients or completed jobs. This taught me heightened levels of responsibility and accountability. My responsibilities were often given to me with a preamble of words meant to convey to me how important my job position was; "You are in charge. You have to take the lead. Make sure everything is done before we get home." 'You're in charge, take the lead' - was the beginning of my relationship with unwanted responsibility and what I saw as the burden of imposed leadership.

After so many years of being the leader by default, I was determined to not add any extra to my plate for a good portion of my life. Even though I wasn't looking for extra, I was governed by a strong sense of responsibility and accountability to my word, my family, and my purpose. My parents instilled in my brothers and me the importance of family, the value of truth, and the honor of my word. They also taught us good communication skills, a strong work ethic, and the pride you take in delivering quality work. For this reason, my moral compass is set high and has prevented me from walking away from responsibility even though it would have been easier in many instances. I am a natural leader.

A strong sense of purpose and well-developed leadership skills has led me to serve organizations and individuals with passion and heart. Purpose has led me to found a nonprofit organization focused on developing and equipping the next generation of leaders with ethics, integrity, empathy, and compassion. These guiding principles have helped me to be courageous even when I was fearful or in times of uncertainty. This early introduction to leadership has been the beacon of light that I have followed through my own life and sought to impress upon my students and clients over the years. I realized that the confidence of these skills has allowed me to walk in truth, and walking in truth has given me a certain freedom that many leaders don't get to experience.

This freedom has helped to keep me honest and in my purpose. It's helped me to walk away from situations and positions that I felt were a threat to the freedom of my spirit and to the ethics and truth I've chosen to uphold. It's also allowed me to walk away from people and relationships that looked good on paper but were detrimental in reality. My spirit has always been my guide. Its desire to be free and happy has always kept me from lingering in spaces, places, or relationships too long. That freedom has played a big part in the writing of this book. There is a peace and confident power that comes from operating from a space of integrity and truth. My desire is that other leaders will also experience this type of freedom, and be released from the oppressive fetters of appearance and false imagery of what leadership has become in far too many instances.

As I continue to work in the Leadership Development field and write this book, I have been surprised by the number of people who are obviously leaders and/or in leadership positions that do not consider themselves to be leaders. I am actually astounded when time and time again people tell me; "I'm not a leader" or "I don't consider myself a leader". This has led me to dissect leadership positions and mentalities around the world and made me realize that too many leaders are graduates of the fake-it-till-you-make-it university; drowning in baptism by fire or leading by default without the grace of being properly equipped and trained. They are left to figure it out as they go along, unable to question, show weakness, or expose the truth of the corruption of their office. Whether your leadership consists of managing a home or a corporation, adhering to principles and a strong sense of identity will help you overcome these challenges.

As an advisor to numerous leaders in business, education, government, and religious sectors, I have seen firsthand, people who were beyond skilled to carry out the technicalities of their duties; yet, they have no clue how to balance or manage their lives outside of those tasks. I've witnessed leaders burn out due to a lack of support from those closest to them. Often, feeling betrayed by their "supporters" unwillingness to see them as human or from their inability to allow anyone else to see them as less than superhuman. I've experienced leaders making tragic mistakes, yet completely unwilling to accept responsibility for their choices. And I've watched as inexperienced leaders were buried under the weight of mismanagement and lack of guidance… and so much more.

So many leaders have been failed by their respective systems and been set up to fail by their predecessors. Those leaders that came before them and were duty-bound to prepare them to succeed by teaching them, guiding them, and directing them through the peaks and valleys of their position, but didn't. Thus, leaving their replacements with undue stress and a lack of proper integration into leadership. Unfairly setting them up for failure and creating space for them to shirk their responsibilities, lead without integrity, operate unethically, and throw compassion and humanity out the door. This is unacceptable!

My desire for this book and you as a reader is that it will help create a space of vulnerability, self-awareness, and compassion for yourself and others. That in reading these letters, you will be able to see yourself and those around you. May these letters help you to truthfully evaluate where you are in relation to where you are going. I believe that wherever you are in your leadership journey, these letters will help you to take inventory of why you are leading and what type of legacy you wish to leave as a leader. These letters are personal. I hope that the words on these pages will inspire you to lead with compassion, integrity, ethics, truth, and love. May your truth guide you, may your heart lead you, and may love light your way Dear Leader!

Table of Contents

Introduction

Dear Leader,

Leadership around the world is in a terrible state. Too many leaders have proven to be ill-equipped, apathetic, self-serving, and power-hungry. Whether they are self-appointed or elected, they have shown themselves to be incapable of carrying out the job for which they have been chosen. From the political arena to the pulpit, people have been made to suffer under faulty leadership and left to wonder who will be their champion, their savior from the mess that has been created.

The state of current leadership has been the result of unethical, ill-prepared, morally compromised, and spiritually bankrupt men and women who have chosen their own interests and advancement ahead of the people they have been commissioned to lead, serve, and protect. They have repeatedly ignored their duties and even their own promises in order to satiate their quest for money, fame, and power. To say that they have been derelict in their duties would be putting it mildly. They have been woefully negligent, callous and compromising at every turn. Unfortunately, to the detriment of every social, economic, educational, religious, and governmental system around the world and society at large. It is safe to say that nearly every aspect of human life has been affected!

Many so-called leaders have made a career of disseminating false information and peddling panic to the masses as a means to stay in power and keep confusion and chaos prevalent in the world landscape. Misinformation and lack of proper preparation and training continues to perpetuate this scheme. They have proven fearful of taking a stand against injustice and popular opinion for fear of criticism, and have sustained the status quo in order to maintain popularity. They have allowed themselves to be muted lest they upset the powers that be. The impotent and flaccid nature of today's leadership has created a self-perpetuating cycle of the same. Leaving us with what may seem a hopeless situation. WHEN will it end? WHAT will turn it around?

WHO will be "the one" to transform it all? What if the answer is closer than you think? What if the answer is YOU?!

Fortunately, the weight of transforming the world doesn't rest on your shoulders alone. This is a clarion call to all leaders past, present, and future to stand up and refuse to continue to allow the spirit of mediocrity, greed, and apathy to be the breast at which our leadership is suckled. Waiting for a hero does not and has not worked. No one can do this alone. But if those who have done it well don't share their wisdom, and those that are doing it now don't look for and listen to their wisdom, then those that are coming will be doomed to struggle and fail just as we have been failed.

Identity

"Never forget what you are, for surely the world will not. Make it your strength. Then it can never be your weakness. Armor yourself in it, and it will never be used to hurt you."

— George RR Martin

Dear Leader,

WHO ARE YOU? Do you know? We understand that you have a title, and maybe a job that merits the utilization of that title to describe all or some of the capacity in which you may perform a duty. But that tells us nothing of who you are. We understand your title signifies the hours you've worked, tests you've taken, and sacrifices made to be "recognized"; yet, who are you? Who you are has little if anything to do with your title or influence, and everything to do with your character, ideas, thoughts, and spirit. It is the very essence of your presence. Who you are has everything to do with your core beliefs, attitudes, and actions stemming from them. Do you know the true root of your being? Who and what has shaped who you are at this very moment? Your real why? I often tell my young son "The true you is who you are when no one can see you." When no one is looking, who are you and how do *you* define you? What is your personal identity? What is your identity as a leader?

What is identity? The Cambridge dictionary defines identity as; 1. who a person is or the qualities of a person or group that make them different from others; 2. the reputation, distinguishing characteristics of a person that makes the public think about them in a particular way. These commonly used definitions seem to be based primarily on the way you appear in others' eyes and how they perceive you. But what about how you perceive yourself?

I am writing to you because at least a portion of you identifies as a Leader. Whether you chose or were chosen, someone is looking to you for guidance and inspiration. Most people have preconceived ideas of what you should look like and how you should perform as a leader. You may find yourself living out the ideas of who you are based on someone else's terms and standards, without knowing or having any real connection for yourself. If you don't establish your own identity based on a clear understanding of the experiences, beliefs, wounds, and influences that have contributed to who you are, you will find yourself in a constant state of seeking validation from outside sources. Why does this even matter? It matters because you matter, your leadership matters. What you do and how you do it will affect not only your own life and legacy, but also the lives and legacies of those you come into contact with. If you are oblivious to your who and why, you can do unnecessary and irreparable damage. Is that what you really want to do?

Have you ever asked yourself how your identity was formed? Do you have multiple identities? Does your identity change in the midst of pressures from other people's behaviors or ideas? Do you have a problem being different and standing out? I know this barrage of questions may seem like too many to start our relationship with, but it is only an effort to help you to clarify your relationship with yourself. My questions are purely for the purpose of establishing a foundation on which to build the rest of our conversation; your conversation as a leader.

Great and memorable leaders have one major thing in common, a willingness to go against the grain and in many instances to do something that is not popular or has never been done before. They are often full of unique conversations, ideas and actions; many of which are unfamiliar or not easily understood. They have been subjected to ridicule, loneliness, and rejection. People often try to define them based on the limited scope of their own experiences and education. Even amidst these circumstances, they refuse to cave into the views of others. They carry with them such a strong sense of WHO they are and the gifts they carry, that they are undeterred by the noise and popular language of people around them. You are no less capable than they are. You are no less unique and gifted than them. The question is, are you willing to do the work to discover who you truly are, in order to *be* who you are purposely designed to be?

Purposely? Oh, you thought you were here by accident or by your own making? This may come as a surprise, but that couldn't be further from the truth. You were born for exactly this time in the world. You are here for *such a time as this.* Your unique character, personality, quirks, and ideas are all essential to the accomplishment of your purpose. A purpose that involves impacting humankind. Only when you have a firm and clear view of yourself will you know "*the what*" you are here to contribute. The "what" can range from a cause to a kingdom. However, there is no "what", without a who; so WHO ARE YOU?

Do you spend time with yourself meditating on your existence as a Divine Being connecting with the spirit of your Creation? Do you take time to know yourself, your limits, your flaws, your strengths, and your weaknesses? Are you honest about your breaking points, your deal breakers and your breakdowns (*triggers*)? We all have them. The more honest we are with ourselves about who we are, what we value, and how we operate, the less of a threat outside forces will be to our ideas of who we are; our personal identity. We are then able to walk forward courageously because we are not hiding from the scrutiny of people who don't have a clue about who we are truly designed to be. Don't carry the burden of other people's definition of you. Don't allow yourself to be defined by only a portion of you. When you know yourself, you are not bothered by the definition of you by people that don't know the purpose of you.

"Lions are not concerned with the opinions of sheep"
— Game of Thrones

Your life mission is a never-ending journey of discovery. Discovering what though? Some might believe it's a journey of discovering the wonders of the Universe when in actuality, it's discovering the wonders of you; a divinely created being with a unique contribution to this world. There are levels to discovery. You will acquire the wisdom of each level as you go through the experiences presented within them. I feel that life is like a video game. You start out as a novice, not knowing much, a bit clumsy until you get the hang of it. You face challenges that are equal to your skillset until you master them and advance to the next level. Usually, you advance to the next level after making significant and costly mistakes. Once you have learned to avoid and defeat the challenges, then you are elevated. When you go to the next level you face new challenges in addition to the old ones. The old challenges haven't gone away, you've simply honed your ability to recognize and avoid them. Now you are tasked with mastering the new set of challenges. And so life and discovery go...again and again and again until you've mastered each level.

A fundamental part of mastery is the ability to analyze and know yourself, your strengths, and your weaknesses. To see you. The more you are able to see yourself, the more you will connect with your position in this universe as an intentional creation and contributor to mankind. The more transparent and open you are willing to be about all aspects of you, the deeper the level of your encounter with yourself and with God. His presence within you and in your life will become that much more apparent as you uncover your own greatness. Your gifts and talents are evidence of your greatness. Your job in this lifetime is to share those gifts in service to humanity. Be prepared to continually be asked; "Who are you? Who are you serving? How are you serving?" Though the questions remain the same, the answers will vary based on what stage of discovery you are in. Be willing to grow, revise, and transform along the way.

Elements of Identity

The cycle of learning your identity is constant. There are dimensions to your identity, so much more than your name, title, or vocation. Those are simply masks that we use to be presentable, understandable, or bearable to others who try to perceive us. Maneuvering the dimensions of your identity is like attending a University to acquire a specific degree. While your degree may be in one field of study, it requires learning and comprehension of different related subjects, and how these minor subjects factor into your major. You can't become a doctor without first learning chemistry, biology, and anatomy. We are all students in the University of Life. We spend semesters trying to figure out our major (purpose). Some of us enter the university of life sure that we are meant to be one thing and that one thing will bring us happiness and fulfillment. While you may be fortunate enough to become that *thing*, you may find out that it is only a stepping stone to access a higher purpose.

The universe is neither flat nor one-dimensional. It will serve you well to remember that you are as multifaceted and multi-dimensional as the world in which you live.

Own Yourself

WHO ARE YOU? Don't be afraid to own who and what you are. You have been gifted with many talents and creative insights. Yet I hear you speak of yourself as if you were speaking of a stranger. You talk about your accomplishments from the lens of those who watch you. As the vision and not the visionary. Too many times I've heard you speak to your success and character as if it's an out-of-body experience. Whispering in false humility for fear of being seen as too much. Disconnected from your gifts and oblivious to just how amazing you are. Your favorite phrase is "so I have been told". When will you not need the opinions of outsiders to feel the validation of who you are? When will the need to know what others think of you take a backseat to what you think of yourself?

In order to own who you are, you must know who you are. You will be a different version of yourself in different seasons. You may not always like the version that you see. Own it anyway. Acknowledging and embracing the not so wonderful parts of yourself is an important part of self-awareness. When you realize that you are multidimensional and take time to recognize every aspect of yourself - good, bad, and ugly, you set a firm foundation for your identity. When your personal identity is set on a firm foundation, your tendency to act as you *think* you should be will lessen, and instead, you will actually *be* who you are naturally, without anxiety, doubt, or pressure. Who are you? How do you know? What is your purpose? Where do you find it? Each of us must embark on our own mission to discover our individual calling.

Self-awareness and a strong personal identity will give birth to self-confidence. Observers may interpret your confidence and unwillingness to be defined or controlled as arrogance. To some degree, it may be but in most cases, it isn't. You have been conditioned to believe that the only way to be humble and Godly is to deny who you are, and hide what gifts and talents you bear so as not to appear haughty and overconfident. I challenge that thinking with prejudice. What if one of the godliest things that you can do, aside from loving your neighbors, is to love yourself by acknowledging who you are and how you have been gifted. What if God wants you to know Him and how close He is to you, but the only way to do that is to acknowledge Him in you? Can you see your Divine gifts? Can you see God in those gifts? Can you see God in you? How can you begin to do this? If you have ever appreciated another person's talent or a knack for something - playing an instrument, speaking, singing, sports, writing, and acknowledged it as a God-given ability, then you have already begun. That is also how you can begin to see God in your own gifts and talents. Acknowledge them. In this manner, you will begin to see God in yourself.

Know Thyself

To truly know yourself, you must know what centers you. Who are you at your core? Core knowledge is based on your personal morals, ethics, and integrity. This is the internal homing beacon that shapes your principles and life philosophies. This is your guide to what you view as right or wrong. This is how you classify your value system and determine your boundaries and limits. This is the anchor that holds you in place when things around you are uncertain; when people around you are transient; when shades of grey are the only colors you see. This is your home. Unfortunately, you've been treating your "home" like a rental property. You may visit, but never establish residency, so you never achieve a sense of ownership - and it shows. When you don't establish ownership over yourself, you leave the responsibility of your care and self-worth in the hands of strangers. Imagine owning a piece of property and allowing your neighbors to make the rules for how you can decorate, what it should look like, and when you can use it. You would find that idea absurd, yet that's exactly how many of us are operating in terms of our lives and personas, like tenants instead of owners. Allowing other people's values, ideals, and ethics to govern you is essentially turning over the keys to your home - you. Keep your keys!

Another aspect of self-knowledge is becoming acquainted with the ever-evolving version of you. This is the part of you that is constantly learning, adapting, and growing. The part of you that houses your knowledge, experiences, gifts, and talents. This is the part of you that seeks purpose. The part that knows you have relevance and desires to validate that by discovering and defining that purpose for you. You may see yourself as a simple two-dimensional being who can only manage *being* one thing at a time. This train of thought has been perpetuated for generations through our very limited educational, financial, and social systems. Our grandparents were taught to get a job and stay until retirement. Our parents were taught to get an education, a career, and work sixteen-hour days to be deemed successful. What have you learned? What will you teach?

Please take the time to ask yourself the questions in these letters as a means to help clarify who you are for yourself. As you continue to become reacquainted with yourself, again and again, you will encounter a you that you never knew existed.

You may struggle for years or even a lifetime to find out who you are. Until you establish who you are, you may create a public image based on what you think you know or who you think others believe you to be. You then get upset when "they" don't buy the identity you are trying to sell; when in reality, you don't buy it yourself because you haven't taken the time to connect with your source to actually see what and who you are made to be. It is only when you don't know yourselves that you can be shaken by the opinions of people who have no clue who you are. Know thyself.

Know Your Gifts

Believe me, you have them. Some gifts are obvious, some are hidden, some are unwanted. Whatever the case, they are yours and have been given to you so that you may impact the lives around you. Find them. Use them. Share them. Gifts unused are worse than gifts misused.

A man's gifts maketh room for him and bringeth him before great men.

— Proverbs 18:16

Your gifts make you the answer to someone's prayers and problems. Solving problems will set a stage for your gifts to be on display. The better you are at giving your gifts, the more you will be sought out and the greater your influence. Administer with love and compassion. Integrity and good character will amplify your talents and elevate your worth. Don't allow your character to hinder your gifts. Your gifts will take you far, but it's your character that will keep you there and elevate you further.

Know Your Worth

Do you know your worth? The truth is that you may have to find it first. Though knowing our worth should be innate, it generally is not. Even when we appear to live blessed and charmed lives, many of us still struggle with the actual purpose of our presence in this world. What value do we contribute to validate our existence? More frequently than not, we choose to answer that question based on some one-size-fits-all chart that claims money, fame, and power as the metric of our worth. In order to answer the question of your worth, you must uncover your true identity -not just in the physical, but in the spiritual as well. An identity that says you are worthy because you were created, and that you were created for a purpose.

I have been on the journey of a lifetime and still continue to find new avenues of expression for my gifts. I'm always venturing to push the envelope and stretch the borders of my existence. In my effort to discover purpose, I met a version of me that I never knew existed. A version of me that has been able to achieve things far past my personal level of education or understanding. Past my belief in what I thought was realistic for me to do. Past the impact, I ever imagined being able to have. Through continuing on this path, my vision has been reshaped and expanded. Purpose and Vision are mainstays of leadership. Who or what is shaping your vision? Who or what has defined purpose to you and for you?

Vision and Purpose

"Where there is no vision, there is no hope"

— George Washington Carver

Dear Leader,

What is your vision? To determine the answer to this question you must understand the meaning of vision. Vision is *sight, the ability to see, powers of observation, perception, perspective, view, and the ability to think about or plan the future.* Your vision is important because what you see will determine what you do. *Where is your focus?* What you perceive will be determined by your perspective and your observation abilities. *What is your position?* What you are able to observe is determined by your field of vision. *What is in your line of sight? Is your view obstructed?* Your range of vision is determined by your actual ability to see. *Are you short-sighted or can you see into the distance?*

Where there is no vision, the people perish...Proverbs 29:18

If you do not have a vision for your life you will find yourself wandering aimlessly and toiling in futility. You may find yourself busy making a living, acquiring material things, and yet still feeling unfulfilled and void of purpose. These things are distractions that only delay your discovery of your purpose. To begin to discover purpose, you must first have vision; the ability to think about or plan for the future.

Write the vision and make it plain...Habakkuk 2:2

People will always seek to define you and your vision to fit their understanding. If you are not clear about who you are and what your vision is, then people will define who you are for you. They will criticize you for thinking and acting differently than they do. Some criticism will be helpful, while other critiques will be in an effort to push you into conformity.

How do you determine what is constructive criticism and what is a deviation from your vision? It is often hard to know the difference. Why? Because especially now, leaders are creating new ideas, thoughts, and processes at quantum speed. Some are variations of old ideas, but many are never-been-done before revelations. It is human nature to seek to categorize and define things we see and experience. It helps us to maintain a grasp of reality or an illusion of control. The truth is, however, the more we seek to conform and define things based on old standards, the more we stifle our creativity and limit our expression of an innovative new idea based on our own unique gifts, talents, and perspectives. Creating from a place that has never been touched or exposed before often leaves us vulnerable to the opinions of others. If you do not have a firm grasp on your personal identity, a clear vision, and an understanding of the purpose of your vision, these opinions will knock you off your path. Your vision may be difficult to explain to others, but you need to be sure to define it for yourself.

You will be told your vision needs to be clear, sometimes it just isn't. In those times, be sure to sharpen the vision by writing it down. Speak it as many times as needed to keep it at the forefront of your mind. Don't be deterred by those who don't get it. The vision was given to you for a reason. Keep seeking, keep moving forward to bring it into existence.

On Purpose

I had spent a lifetime feeling as if I had no real purpose or direction/passion. I didn't and still don't have that "thing" that keeps me awake at night or wakes me up in the morning. So much so, that one day I confessed to a friend of mine that I was afraid that I didn't have a passion. She laughed and said; "You most definitely have a passion and it's obvious! Your passion is people and helping them to be better." She said it so plainly and matter-of-factly that I was able to receive that statement as truth. When I was able to accept that my passion didn't manifest the way people said it should, I was released from the burden of finding a box to fit myself and my passion into. I no longer used sleepless nights and fanatical obsession as the gauge to measure the value of my purpose work.

Can you relate to this? Have you been told to find your *one thing* and that will be the thing that you are meant to do for the rest of your life? That finding this elusive one thing will provide you with the satisfaction and fulfillment that you so desire. Do you feel like you've experienced more anxiety around finding that thing than actually living and doing what you are doing at present? What if I were to tell you that purpose isn't one space in time in your life nor is it one cause to champion, but instead, a state of being that changes and evolves as you do? What if your purpose is simply being the best version of you possible at any given time. What if being the best version of you guided you into compassionate, loving, and service-filled actions toward your fellow man?

Purpose is not a one-stop-shop. I believe that we confuse the gifts and talents we have and how we utilize them as the definition of our purpose. My belief is that we all have the same purpose - you don't have to agree with me, but please hear me out. I believe that our job in this lifetime is to discover the truth of who we are, and wholeheartedly acknowledge and embrace the unique gifts and talents with which we have been endowed. Once we accept our individuality and these gifts, then we are to utilize these gifts in service of humanity. We are to use our unique character and experiences to share our knowledge and assist others to do the same. You will have different expressions of your gifts and talents throughout your lifetime. How you use those gifts during those times will help in your evolution and become a part of your legacy.

Character

Character is both formed and revealed by how one deals with everyday situations as well as extraordinary pressures and temptations. Like a well-made tower, character is built stone by stone, decision by decision

– **Michael Josephson**

Dear Leader,

What is the quality of your character? Do you know? Character in short is your reputation. It's how you respond to a situation when you have power and when you don't. It's how you treat people with money and without. It's your response when you are under pressure and stress. It's what you do when no one can see you. Character is the house of your morals, ethics, and integrity. Your character will influence how you make decisions and plays a significant role in how you are perceived and received as a leader. Your level of commitment to be moral and ethical is grounded in your values. When you live out your values your decisions will reflect that. What do you value? You must define it for yourself. What have you been taught to value? Your leadership style will bear witness to it.

In a world where you can virtually be anybody, are you who you say you are? You may have witnessed the advancement and influence of people who appear to be one way, only to discover that they are far from their public persona. Is that you? Are you for sale to the highest bidder in order to satiate your unquenchable thirst to be popular or seen as desirable? Do you live in bondage to the alter ego that you have sold to us, your followers?

Character is often forged in the fires of life. Those times when you are in a space to make pivotal decisions are often where you add the bricks of strong character. These are the moments when your decisions will indicate the path you will continually follow. Remember this as you go along. Though you may have the opportunity to course-correct later, some corrections are much harder to make farther down the road...and much more costly.

Accountability

Dear Leader,

Does your fear of being wrong and a desire to be perfect paralyze you from actually making decisions and taking action? Are you allowing fear of criticism to hold you hostage in a state of lukewarm hesitancy, leaving the people following you confused and uncertain? Has your fear of making any choice earned you the reputation of being fickle and untrustworthy? Trust is hard to come by and people want to trust their leaders. One of the most important characteristics of a good leader is surety and confidence. Surety does not mean having all the right answers or never making a mistake. It simply means being ready to take action and to be willing to accept responsibility for what those actions produce. That's where many leadership dilemmas begin. I am of the opinion that accountability has been replaced to a large degree by the ability and desire to finesse people and situations. Holding people accountable seems to be exceptionally challenging in modern society. I believe people want to be accountable but are often scrutinized to such a high degree that they fear nothing they do will be right or satisfactory. The idea of rejection can deter even the bravest of us. News flash, you can't and you won't satisfy everybody.

Unfortunately, our society has become full of emotionally charged, hair-trigger-mob-mentality-overly-sensitive people who no longer look for truth or verification of truth before they crucify. This makes putting ourselves in the eye of public scrutiny even harder to manage.

In this manner, we are not far removed from our old close-minded ancestors and forefathers that burned people at the stake and showed up with pitchforks and torches to punish those deemed different, weird, or nonconforming. The only difference now is that instead of actual lynching we perform public and social lynching. Due to the nature of social media and the speed at which information travels, we are quick to play judge and jury over people's lives for any offense perceived or real. The verdicts are usually swift and merciless. I've seen so many people convicted in the court of popular opinion based only on a well-placed picture and caption. No context, no investigation, no proof - only the opinions formed from interpretations of a snapshot of information. This is scary. I've often been personally frustrated by the willingness of people to be so easily led and their unwillingness to research and confirm information for themselves. It pains me to see how unwilling to forgive or show compassion we as a society have become. It's easy for anybody to be harsh from behind a wall of anonymity.

It's no wonder that you have social anxiety and worry that your thoughts and words can and will be misconstrued at the whims of people that are ignorant of who you are and the truth of your heart.

This can be exceptionally challenging for the Leader that has a heart of service but is not anchored in identity, vision, and purpose. How can you manage this rough terrain? Here are 2 keys: Accountability and word management. When most folks hear the word accountability, they hear a set up for blame and fault finding. While there will always be someone willing to find fault with what you do or don't do, you have the ability to override this with your willingness to be accountable for what you say and what you do. Having a support team to provide checks and balances will do much to keep you accountable, but ultimately it's your job to manage you.

The second key is word management. Watch your mouth! I'm sure you have probably heard the wise advice to think before you speak. Do that! A leader governed by their emotions and ego very seldom takes time to think about what they are saying before they say it. The results can range from mild embarrassment to complete devastation. You have no doubt seen someone's words come back to bite them and wreak havoc on their relationships, their brands, or their business. In the age of hot mics and leaked recordings, it is sage advice to be mindful of the words you speak. We all have conversations that are not necessarily for the general public. However, if those conversations are based on gossip, deceit, or hurtfulness consider whether or not you are prepared to accept the fallout from the words that fall out of your mouth.

> *Death and life are in the power of the tongue: and*
> *they that love it shall eat the fruit thereof.*
> — **Proverbs 18:21**

I could write endlessly about the power of words, but I won't. What I will do is make a few very important points for you to consider. Your words are powerful, more powerful than you know. The words you speak effectively create the reality that you live in. If your words are full of venom and vitriol, you will be guaranteed to be surrounded by the same. Your words create your world. Even the seemingly harmless popular words carry weight. Be mindful. What are you speaking over yourself- sickness, poverty, death? What are you speaking over those around you, your family, your children? Most supposed curses that we experience are merely self-fulfilling prophecies that stem from the careless way we pronounce things over ourselves. What does your world look like right now? You probably spoke it.

My next point is about the power of *your* word. There was a time when a person's word was their bond. The only contract needed was the knowledge that a word was spoken. We are so far removed from that type of integrity, that it's even hard for people to honor their word on legal contracts. Even so, that doesn't mean that you can't be a person of your word. What does your word mean when spoken? Does it elicit trust and confidence or doubt and suspicion? Are you deceitful and double-minded? Do you speak with a forked tongue? Have you even thought about it? I hope that you have chosen to build a legacy of honesty and that as a leader you are trustworthy with your work and your word. If you haven't, it may be time to take inventory of yourself and your leadership. Your underlings and followers are watching and imitating what you do *and* what you say. You have the power to charge and change the environment you are in. It starts at the top. What are you trickling down?

Dear Leader

WHO ARE YOU?

WHAT ARE YOUR GIFTS?

WHAT IS YOUR VISION?

WHAT PURPOSE ARE YOU SERVING AT THIS TIME IN YOUR JOURNEY?

WHO ARE YOU ACCOUNTABLE TO?

WHAT IDENTITY HAVE YOU OR DO YOU DESIRE TO ESTABLISH?

Challenges

"When we least expect it, life sets us a challenge to test our courage and willingness to change; at such a moment, there is no point in pretending that nothing has happened or in saying that we are not yet ready. The challenge will not wait. Life does not look back."

— **Paulo Coelho**

Dear Leader,

Some days you will feel like you absolutely cannot breathe. You will be in the midst of a dilemma that perplexes and frustrates you. On one hand, you will have things happening that will tell you that you are moving forward, advancing and that things are working out. At the same time, you may be experiencing being inundated with the blows of life. You find yourself treading virtual water, trying to stay afloat and keep the faith; unable to register gratitude quick enough to conquer the feeling of "*What the Hell?*" that comes from everything happening at once. You will feel lost, confused, frustrated and angry.

I have been there many times, and the feelings have usually come right at the tail end of a seemingly amazing win. I successfully launched my first international leadership academy session in South Africa in February 2018. Prior to the launch in February, my youngest son was an innocent victim of gun violence four days before Christmas. He spent a week in the ICU and I stayed by his side the whole time. The day I brought him home from the hospital my mother informed me that she had been diagnosed with stomach cancer - Stage 4. Little did I know that this was to be the beginning of a year of trials. By the time March rolled around, my life was a wreck and the hits just kept on coming. Seven days after my triumphant return from South Africa, I was homeless. For 30 days, where I would be sleeping on a near-daily basis was in question. My foundation was rocked!

After 30 days of homelessness, I found a home. A week after I moved into my new place (victory), I learned that my father's battle with diabetes had progressed to heart and kidney failure and required hospitalization. I could barely breathe as each new blow knocked me down and overshadowed my victories as quickly as they came. I was overwhelmed, drowning, and barely holding on to my sanity let alone my purpose. I couldn't function. I had to check out in order to go on. I had to be ok with not being okay. I had to be willing to tell people around me that I was drowning and that I needed to process what was happening. I was exhausted mentally and physically. My weight was climbing steadily, I was fatigued, my body ached, and my mind lingered in a state of constant fog. I knew that if I didn't sit down, I wouldn't be able to move forward.

You will have these times if you haven't already, and some of the keys to getting through it will be to have compassion for yourself and to be willing to take time out from being "super" in order to regenerate. Many of us are under the false assumption that if we slow down, someone else will beat us to our destiny. Please know what's yours, is yours. Your destiny is not for sale. You dictate the speed and direction of your travel. You may believe that taking a break is an impossibility and that the desire to take a break is a sign of weakness. It takes courage to admit vulnerability. When the time comes, however many times it comes up, choose your health and well-being. It takes courage to be honest about your emotions. Be courageous.

As I was going through my trials, I chose to be courageous and vulnerable. I told my close friends that I wasn't ok. I shared with them that I was confused, exhausted, and in need of rest. Even though I thought I was speaking clearly about my emotional and mental status, it was still hard for them to grasp the depth of what I was trying to convey. I was the one that usually had the answers; the strong one. Though they had never seen me in this state, they still provided a space for me to work through my challenges without judgment or rejection. I was grateful. Still, my life felt like a jigsaw puzzle that was missing essential pieces. Why weren't they getting it, and why couldn't I get out of it? Because I was being *logical* about my emotions. I was self-diagnosing and self-treating. I was minimizing my emotions amid my crisis. I had simplified my feelings to a description - *frustrated*. I thought I was only dealing with frustration. It took a close friend pressing me for an answer to help me get to the core of my emotions. She asked me point blank; " Are you *angry*? Are you angry at God?" It was then that I realized I was in fact *pissed off*! No wonder I wasn't getting any relief. I wasn't even addressing the real problem. As the realization of my true emotions crept over my mind and began to register, my body suddenly felt lighter and an instant shift occurred. In that moment, I felt a sense of liberation at being able to acknowledge that I was worried and angry that I was worrying over stuff I shouldn't have had to worry about! My situation had not changed, but my overview of what I was going through, and the emotions that were attached to it had.

What did I learn from this time in my life? I learned several things that I hope will help you.

1. Acknowledge life and the things that are happening as they happen. Do not ignore failures, disappointments, losses, challenges, or pain. They are real and they have an impact on your ability to function. Trying to "tough it out" will only last so long and you will eventually have to face the reality of those suppressed emotions.

2. It's ok to take a time-out, even if people around you don't understand or want you to. Only you can decide what is best for you. Choose your sanity and your health over pleasing the masses.

3. It's important to have a good inner circle. People who will love you and support you and your choices, even when they don't understand them. The people closest to you don't have to "get" everything that you do, they just need to trust and love you.

On Fatigue

Dear Leader,

In this current fast-paced society that is steadily picking up speed, it can be difficult to find the time and space to relax. Maybe you want to rest, but in many instances, you lack the ability to shut-down in order to receive that rest. You have been programmed to believe that *hard* work, not just work, is the only way to success. You worry that if you take time away from working, you will fall behind or worse yet, fail. You may believe that whatever needs to be done, *needs* to be done by you. Have you been going nonstop with the hopes that all your incessant running will somehow get you to your intended goal quicker? Are you exhausted? Do you know the cost of exhaustion?

Striving to acquire things and keep up with what popular culture dictates will also lead to success fatigue. If you examine what you are working towards, you may begin to see that you often spend a large portion of your time alienating the families and loved ones that you claim to be doing it all for. You lose the meaningful connections and joyful experiences you dream of. You've acquired the titles, gadgets, and accolades, yet you still are not happy.

I'm definitely not saying that hard work and dedication doesn't pay off, they do, but I'm questioning what it has cost you? What has been the trade-off? What have you lost? Many successful and influential people will tell you about the great rewards of going nonstop like the energizer bunny; however, they neglect to speak about the carnage of what they left behind or lost, and at what personal cost. Because they lacked balance in their pursuit, they've lost loves, lost friendships, lost families, and even lost themselves. What they won't tell you about is the need for constant validation from outside sources in the form of accolades, titles, and material possessions to make them feel valued and seen. Why? Because despite all of their victories, they may have lost the ability to see themselves and the fact that they deserve to be cared for. They may not register how much they neglect themselves.

On a more personal note, the fatigue caused by striving for success can also cost you your compassion. You may find yourself too tired to be kind, too tired to be considerate, too tired to have empathy, too tired to be patient... with yourself as well as others. I can say from personal experience that being just regular every day tired has seen my patience tested. Add in exhaustion and I've spoken unkind words just because they were quicker to say and required no thought or consideration. I've been impatient, snappy, and exacerbated. Have you ever done that? Success fatigue can look like, but not be limited to a constant state of anger. Are you mad all of the time? Due to the demands you have placed on yourself, you may feel resentment for the pressure you feel to continually perform. That resentment may extend to the recipients of the spoils of your success due to their expectations of you. You may view them as ungrateful because of this; not recognizing that *you* were the architect of their expectations. They treat you as you have trained them to treat you.

Maybe it's time to train people to treat you differently, starting with yourself. Be kind to you first. Examine your motives and evaluate your current status. Check your emotions. This may help you determine the cause of your overwhelm. It might be time to release some things so that you can enjoy your success. Maybe it's time to pause and prioritize so that you remember what is important. Breathe.

Sometimes you don't realize you weren't breathing until you actually take a breath.

Identity Crisis – DNA

To sustain what we are fighting for, we must be
clear about what we are fighting against. Is it
physical, mental, or spiritual? Is it generational or
created from our present activities?
Each of us has an internal battle that is waged in
our minds and our spirit. The DNA that created you
also bequeathed to you a pre-existing war that will
be yours to fight until you win or lose.

Dear Leader,

You were born in an uncertain time. Maybe finances were tight, relationships were strained and the prospects of the future looked cloudy. There were questions around your viability. Were you wanted? Would you survive? Yet, despite any odds that were not in your favor you prevailed. You won over those opposing forces and made it here. You were born full of promise and purpose. From your beginning, you stood out for your unique characteristics - physically, mentally, and maybe even spiritually.

Life for you changed abruptly at an early age, through no fault of your own, still, you were deeply wounded. How deeply, no one knew, not even you. At that space in time, you made the decision to protect yourself from everything and everyone, that people aren't to be trusted; they lie, they wound, they leave. You began to build a fortress around your heart to keep you safe from infiltration by anyone or anything that sought to do you harm. Since you didn't know who was whom, everything sat positioned on your personally constructed chopping block waiting for the slightest hint of betrayal to be cut off.

Your exterior became tougher and tougher to penetrate, even for those who love and care for you. In your mind, your stoicism was the only protection you had. Trust no one, protect yourself. To the outside world, you appear arrogant and selfish, maybe even angry and cold. But for you, that is a small price to pay to ensure that the pain you've already experienced or are seeking to avoid will never find you. You refuse to allow even the smallest possibility that fear, rejection, or pain will find a foothold in your life. So the walls get higher and the interior door to your heart closes slowly. Isolation is your friend.

In spite of your walls, you are blessed to be surrounded by people that bring lessons of grace and love. Sources of inspiration, cheerleaders, and mentors who see the light in you and strive to support your success. People who see your strength and will follow you anywhere...if only you would lead. But you don't see it that way. Despite what they say or do, you refuse to break down your barriers to expose your fragile core. They'll only hurt you - so the story goes. You push them away with tears in your soul and decide to do it on your own. You don't even grasp what is happening or the reason why. You are battling the voices of invisible demons. All you hear is; "You're a screw-up! You're stupid. You're worthless. You're a failure!"

The positive words and conversations of those that love you get buried under the negative ones. You can't afford to take any opinions in, good or bad, from anyone lest you be weakened by their words. There is only you. You can only afford to hear you. The only one who cares about you - is you. Add another brick in the wall.

Your frustration grows with yourself. You don't understand what is wrong with you. You just don't know why you can't get it right. Why you make bad choices, why you seem to do the opposite of what is good or good for you. Slowly a crack appears in your psyche and that little whisper begins to speak "Maybe you are like your father. Maybe you are stupid. Maybe you aren't smart enough. Maybe the good in life is only meant for other more deserving people. Maybe your mother was right about you. Maybe you are truly unworthy of happiness, joy, and love. Maybe...

You fight through, on your own, time and time again to bring yourself upright. *You'll show them all!* You wrestle through the crowd with no ability to separate friend from foe. You will strain and break relationships with your disregard for others. There is only you and your struggles that no one understands. Your actions are fueled by the pain that you are trying to hold at bay by running erratically through the maze of life.

Maybe the people who care for you have unresolved anger and fear too. Maybe it has shaped their perspectives and attitudes. They may see actions from you that trigger their own insecurities and fears of failure. It may make them revisit past relationships and heartbreaks that have inflicted the wounds and scars that they carry themselves. Maybe in their effort to protect you (and ultimately themselves) from those hurts, they unwittingly cause a different wounding. A wounding that looks and sounds like rejection, disappointment, abandonment, anger, animosity, and contempt. Please know that whatever has brought you to this stage is no one event, no one mistake, no one person, no one relationship, not just you. You are not the sum of your errors or your successes. You always have the ability and choice to write and rewrite your own narrative. No one has the key to your identity except you and the Source of your origin. Not the one who bore you, but the One who designed you.

My grandfather used to say; "*It doesn't matter what they call you, it only matters what you answer to.*" What have you decided to answer to?

No man is an Island. Though your fortress of independence, self-reliance, and isolation may have served you or still serves you, at some point in life you must realize that an island of "I" cannot be sustained and eventually will prove to be mortal. This mentality has brought you far and taught you many lessons - even protected you from harm in some instances, but eventually, you will need to realize that you weren't meant to do it alone, nor did you. We all get by with a little help from our friends, families, and angels known and unknown.

Please take time in your life to heal the wounds that would have you perform as a one-man show and build barricades around you. The funny thing about walls is that they will not only keep out what is undesirable, they will block out your ability to receive the good things too.

Popularity

Dear Leader,

You're never as good as they say you are, and you're probably not as bad as they say you are either - people are fickle. Don't become a slave to other people's opinions of you. People are always looking for someone to hand the reins to in order to release themselves from the burden of being accountable for the decisions they make and the state of their lives based on those decisions. They want the results, but not the responsibility of the work it takes to get the results. They will gladly crown you as their fearless leader as long as you fit their ideals and fulfill their desires. Yet, these same raving fans will enthusiastically burn you at the stake for the slightest infraction. The cheers of adoration will fade and turn to taunts and cries for your deposition as quickly as the wind blows. So why would you subject yourself to that scrutiny? When scrutiny does arise, you better know why you chose leadership in order to survive whatever tribulation it brings.

I am convinced that one of the biggest reasons people avoid taking the lead is because of this fear of rejection and scrutiny that comes with the job. Being in the front of the pack means that you are subject to everyone watching what you think, what you say, and what you do. Some people will watch you out of simple curiosity and for entertainment purposes. Some will observe you in order to emulate you. Yet others will watch just to critique and find flaws in what you do. Whatever people's reasons, it can create serious performance anxiety and stress for you as a leader. Trying to do a good job, while not always having all the answers, in the midst of friends and foes can be a recipe for disastrous leadership decisions. Are you so consumed with being liked and accepted by everybody that you are easily swayed and distracted by the voices of whoever is loudest, or whoever has your attention at that moment?

Being a leader without a sense of personal identity, a strong moral foundation and your own voice weakens your position, power, and influence. While it is important to receive and evaluate input on matters from outside sources, in the end, a leader has to ultimately rely on their own experiences, values, and gut instincts to make the final decision. Who wants to follow someone who can't or doesn't take a stand for anything, who has no personal beliefs or standards that are apparent to those that are following them. Like the old cliche "If you don't stand for something, you will fall for anything." Are you as fickle as your followers?

As a leader, you will be faced with situations that may challenge your beliefs, ideology, morals, and even your religion. Some of these challenges will result in you changing your position, and that's okay. However, if your position changes depending on who is in front of you, this is a problem. You have to make a choice early on as to what type of leader you desire to be. Will you be a weak-willed puppet that panders to the highest bidder and goes anywhere the crowd dictates? Or will you be a legacy builder who leads from a strong foundation of character, morals, and standards? To be the latter type of leader requires that you know who you are at your core. Having a strong sense of identity will be your guidance system to give you direction no matter what circumstances you find yourself in. You will need this guidance system to be intact in order to get through one of the most difficult challenges of leadership - facing the crowd.

Our current social climate can be compared to that of the Gladiator arenas in Ancient Rome. The stadium is full of spectators looking to be entertained at the expense of others. The crowd applauding the performance of the winning opponent and hissing reproach on the unfortunately defeated; effectively kicking them when they are down. Though the crowd may have favorites, they are only loyal to their own desires and the thrill of victory. Whoever is delivering their desired results is who receives their praise.

You would do well to understand this before seeking to please the crowd. Playing to the crowd may gain you attention and followers, but can do little for you when you are actually in the midst of the fight. Cheers will pump you up, but only your training, skills and experience will help you navigate wins on the battlefield. Prepare well. Do not allow the crowd's praise to lead you to overestimate your competency and cause you to strive to put on a performance for their favor.

The Crowd

You may have watched as I did while various so-called leaders and influencers took center stage in politics and played a seemingly never-ending tennis match between outlandish and unbelievable behavior and conversation. Using their platforms irresponsibly in order to stroke their egos and push their own agendas. During this time we saw divisions run deep through our society like never before. Underlying biases and prejudices came springing to the surface for all to see. People chose sides based on political affiliation, racial groupings, economic status, sexual preference, and any other identifying factors they deemed important. Sensitivities are at an all-time high and manifest in the form of unrealistic ideas of sameness meaning equality - if we all can't have it, then no one can.

As people's voices began to rise to express their opinions, so too did the practice of trying to shut them up. It has become common practice to ostracize and humiliate any person who makes a misstep or whose opinions go against the popular majority. Hyper-sensitivity and willingness to take offense to any and everything leaving people afraid to speak their mind. Silence strengthened by the ever-present threat that anything said or done in your present or past can become the weapon used to undermine your credibility and destroy your reputation. Thus cancel-culture, the erroneous idea that people *are* their mistakes, has gripped our world.

The dangerous rise of cancel-culture has created an environment of people who feel it is ok to disregard and "cancel" people who do not speak in unison with the masses or agree to whatever is popular at the time. I have seen people lose their influence, businesses, and careers for mistakes that could have easily been addressed and overcome through conversation and a little bit of grace. While some may have committed egregious acts on a continual basis, a vast majority of mistakes are based solely on ignorance and immaturity. The idea that a human being should be discarded and erased for their mistakes or for not following the status quo is a recipe for tyrannical and oppressive regime building.

You may one day face the cancel-culture crowd for something you are currently doing, something you've done in your past, or worse yet, an interpretation of something. How will you handle it? Can you handle it? Every situation will be different and require unique individual responses. I can't say exactly how you should face it, but I can give you basic steps to help you as you maneuver it.

1. **Be honest and take ownership - Right or wrong.** I know that PR people will tell you the first move is to distance yourself from the situation. This is a common practice to establish doubt and possibly help you deny involvement. This is deceptive and has helped create the climate of distrust and conspiracy that we are currently experiencing. What would happen if you had a policy of ownership of your actions? Would you possibly be more mindful of the things that you do and say knowing that you will be held accountable?

2. **Offer a sincere apology** - but only if you are really sorry for what you have done and the damage it may have caused. Even if your intentions were good, you may inadvertently cause harm - acknowledge this.

The only sincere apology is changed behavior. If you have already changed your behavior or are in the process, then an apology is welcomed - if not, keep it. More on this in a future letter.

3. **Make amends** - if you made a mistake, FIX IT! Some of the worst feuds and wars could have been squashed with this step. This doesn't mean groveling, but it does mean doing your best to make the person or group you've wronged whole - whatever that looks like.

Please realize that even after you've taken these steps, not everyone will be happy or satisfied with how you've tried to correct your mistake. That's just a fact of life. The greatest peace you will be able to have is if you have done your best to make amends, alter the faulty behavior and continue to not only learn from your mistakes but also share what you've learned to help others avoid making the same mistakes. Sometimes this is the best you will be able to do. Do it.

Preparation and Growth

Unless you try to do something beyond what you have already mastered, you will never grow.

— **Ralph Waldo Emerson**

Dear Leader,

You must be a soldier before you can become a General. Anything worth having takes time, including your position. We live in a world of "Give it to me now". Man's constant appetite for instant gratification has created a culture of impatience and entitlement. We have lost the ability to wait. We have forsaken the importance of taking time and allowing things to mature naturally. We don't respect processes. As a result, we have food that has no nutritional value because it has been processed chemically. We have loss of employment because machines do it faster. We experience leaders with little to no experience in positions of influence, who are leading from *theory* and not experience and wisdom because they were too impatient to wait. Too many people with talent are being put into positions while lacking insight and wisdom.

You can look in any business or industry and find a line of people fighting for position and title, yet not applying that same level of energy to being properly prepared for the responsibilities of the position. Then to add insult to injury, they have the audacity to be arrogant, stubborn, and prideful. Many of these would-be leaders are powerfully gifted and naturally talented. However, they erroneously believe that their gifts and talents are sufficient to carry them through. Many come from the school of fake-it-till-you-make-it and believe this means that getting into the position is all that is required. Instead of seeking the mentorship and guidance to assist them in effectively leading, they attack those around them and dishonor predecessors in order to divert attention from their deficiencies. Some have become disillusioned with the leadership before them because of their lack of guidance. Some may actually be more informed than their elders in certain areas. Yet, this does not negate the value of being advised by someone with more time and experience.

Not every inexperienced leader is terrible at their job, but that doesn't mean they don't need training and direction. The wisest of leaders seek wise counsel. There are some things that only experience can teach. There are some mistakes that only experienced eyes can see. Being properly prepared and guided will fortify you as a leader.

This admonition is not age-specific. Anyone at any time can be an inexperienced leader. If you are in fact learning new things, as you should be, at any time you will be a beginner. The pathway to your success will be your willingness to be coachable as a student and correctable as a leader. Do not allow pride or fear of embarrassment to be the recipe for your downfall. Do not allow your impatience to make you rush into a position that you are not ready for and cause yourself and those you lead undue stress and harm. Learn patience and the power of proper training. Allow yourself to go through the process of preparation and maturation. You will lessen the likelihood of humiliation and failure, and increase the likelihood of your success.

This is not about shutting down the younger generation, this is solely to remind us all of the value of order, mentorship, and respect for the knowledge and wisdom of prior generations. If they experienced it, they have insight into it.

In African culture when an elderly person goes before and leads the way, it is considered a blessing. When a younger person runs ahead and disregards the elder, it is not only considered disrespectful, it disturbs the order of things. Don't disregard wisdom. Don't block your blessing.

On Growth

Dear Leader,

Have you stopped growing? Have you reached such a height that you feel there is no room for your continued growth? Have you become stingy with your gifts and knowledge only doling out minuscule portions that yield worthless fruit? Has your unwillingness to move, grow or share resulted in the stunting of your team, cohorts, or heirs? Has your ego blocked the growth or recognition of the potential in another? Is there a fledgling standing in your shade hoping to catch a glimpse of the greatness you have achieved? Are you so convinced of your superior nature that you hold the reins with your ego and believe they can only rise to the level you see fit? Silently afraid that they will one day surpass you and your accomplishments, refusing to allow them to acquire their own identity or build their own legacy.

I am quite certain that one of the greatest disservices done to potential leaders is the stifling of their identity and talent by would-be mentors and elders. Instead of recognizing and nurturing the gifts within these pupils and encouraging their development, they choose to exploit their talents or break their spirit in an effort to continuously remind the student that they are the Master. I am also convinced that this is the action of a person that has stopped growing and has become attached to and comfortable with the level that they are perched on. So comfortable that they decide they are the metric by which to be measured, and anyone seeking to reach or surpass them must get through them first. They appoint themselves gatekeepers and gods. With this mindset, they consciously or unconsciously interact with those seeking their guidance as subservient or adversarial. How many potential leaders have been crushed by the very person who was assigned to help them grow?

Leadership isn't just about being in front and being seen. True leaders are also masters of replication. Building up and preparing other leaders and successors to lead effectively is a mandate of leadership. Unfortunately, many leaders have missed the memo! No one wants to think of their own mortality, yet the reality is that no one lives forever and eventually someone else will replace us all. No matter what you do or how great you do it, you will not prevent the eventuality of death. I don't mean to be morbid, I am only speaking a fact of life that too many of us seem to have forgotten in our quest to be the best and greatest. There is nothing wrong with wanting to be the best at what you do. The question that must be asked is; "Who did you step on, leave behind, or destroy in the process?"

The sad part of this reality is that a culture of "not enough" and the idea that there can only be one has been perpetuated in our society for so long that most of us have adopted it with no question either in doctrine or practice. This is manifested in two ways. Either you believe that you must be in and maintain the number one position in order to validate your existence, or you believe that there is not enough for you and you are not enough, therefore, you cry or worship at the feet of the "winner". This is an unfortunate fallacy that has taken the shape of a truth; and in so doing has upset the cycle of personal growth and mentorship that is designed to build up support systems of capable leaders.

We are like trees that grow in different seasons and different ways depending on the purpose. Some trees will only reach a certain height but will boast such an extensive root system that even concrete cannot stop its growth. Others will grow so tall that they overshadow everything around them.

There is always discomfort in growth. Are you willing to personally undergo the discomfort of stretching yourself in order to be able to guide other leaders through their growth? Many leaders talk a good game but lack the fortitude required to weather the real storms. I have found that growth is one of the most uncomfortable spaces we can ever be in life. Growth requires more than sacrifice. It often entails a complete stripping of our assumed identity in order to make a way for the real one. Along my path to mastery, my biggest growth spurts have always occurred just behind my biggest periods of challenge and darkness. These are the things most leaders don't speak about. The times when seemingly no one is listening, when ideas refuse to flow. The seasons when no one believes in you or when no one can help you. The willingness to share the ugliest parts of your journey is the mark of a prolific leader. One that doesn't sugar-coat the process to make the outcome appear glamorous; nor try to forget or ignore the wounds inflicted upon you by the snags and bumps in the road you took to get here. Success is born in the struggle. Lack of growth is equivalent to death. Continually seeking and receiving knowledge is key to your evolution as a leader.

On Moving Forward

Dear Leader,

There is a time and a place for everything. Are you in the right place for this time? As a leader, have you felt the anxiety of wondering if it's simply too late and you'll never reach your goal. Do you have regret for missed opportunities and bad choices? As I reflect on my life, I can honestly say that I have felt that way more than once. I can see several periods in time where there was a fork in the road and I wondered what the result would have been if I had chosen the other road.

You might look back at your choices and lament what you think may have been a better deal or outcome. Maybe you believe that the end result would have been better than what you have now, but it also could have turned out far worse than the fantasy you hold about it. This type of fantasizing can leave you filled with remorse that in no way serves or grows you. I offer another perspective with which to view your choices. One that can free you from the paralyzing burden of shame, guilt, and regret. What if you gave yourself credit for making decisions based on who you were and what you knew at the time you made the decisions.

In an effort to make sense of your current situation, you might make the mistake of looking back on yourself and your past decisions with the maturity and understanding of your present self. You bash the current version of yourself for the errors of your past self. You ruminate on your past mistakes with your present wisdom. What if you were graceful with yourself; old and new versions. What if you decided to assess the value of the lessons learned from a narrative of growth instead of judgment? How different would your shame quotient be?

The growth narrative says; "While I cannot change the choices I have made, I can rejoice in the growth I've experienced. I am grateful for the lessons and experiences that have expanded me. I am no longer using the same limited view from the past to make current decisions."

Do you realize you can only see the lack of wisdom in past decisions because of the wisdom gained either by maturity or from making the mistake in the first place? Celebrate - You're still here! Can you look at your life from the perspective of what was gained instead of what was lost - real or imagined? Sometimes changing the perspective of what you look at is all it takes to transform your mind and your life.

Being flexible in how you perceive a thing can save you. As a 2x divorcee - I can promise you that having an altered perspective of my situation is what preserved my sanity and accelerated my healing. Instead of focusing on the loss of the relationship and the pain of failure, I chose to focus on what was gained from the experience. My children became my first focal point. I was able to find joy in knowing that the children that were born because of these partnerships are distinct and unique because of the uniqueness of the parents that created them. If I had not met those exes, if I had not completed those pregnancies - these individuals that I cherish so dearly would not be in existence. Yes, I probably would have had other children, but they would not have been *these* children. What else did I gain? Life-long friendships formed with people I met through my partnerships. Beautiful experiences that are committed to my memory forever. Experiences that have helped form the fabric of my being. It wasn't always bad. I chose to focus on the positive lessons - even in the pain. I reviewed what I had learned. I had definitely learned lessons of self-value. Some of those lessons were:

- People treat you the way you train them to
- People treat you the way you treat yourself

- The power of choice and being accountable for those choices.
- I learned to pay more attention to what people do rather than to what they say (myself included)
- I learned how to leave a situation with grace
- I learned patience and compassion
- I learned forgiveness

For me, these lessons are far more valuable than what it felt like I lost at the time. The time that I thought I lost was really time spent acquiring knowledge that would help me in the future. Because of these experiences, I am able to guide and mentor others through their hardships. I have helped countless women and men to move through and stand firm in their trials because I was willing to have a different perspective about my own experiences.

That's not to say that while I was going through it, I had this clarity and wise verbiage. At the time, I was in tremendous pain and I was simply making choices to try to ease my pain. These choices were based on my experiences and mentality up to that point. I did the best I could with what I had, in order to make the pain stop. My decisions were also based on a lot of intuition. Simply trusting my gut. In the midst of my struggles I often felt abandoned, alone, and uncertain of friendships, love, or the presence of God.

I felt like I couldn't trust anything, so I had to trust myself. I was more interested in ending my own pain than being concerned with someone else's perspective of my situation. I chose me. I only knew my happiness was not going to come through being angry and waiting for someone to save me. The pathway to healing and being able to salvage my sanity was my willingness to honestly acknowledge all of the feelings I felt and process them. I was honest with myself and with the people around me. Regardless of whether or not they agreed with my feelings. I had no desire to sugarcoat or camouflage my pain for anyone.

I share this as one of the *many* instances in my life that required me to choose to shift in order to move forward. Your ability to move forward is dependent on your willingness to shift in order to do so. You are responsible for your own healing and your perspective. You get to choose the narrative; your own or one that is scripted for you.

People will make up stories about who they think you are and what they think your actions and reactions should be. Remember that is for their comfort-not yours.

Dear Leader

HOW ARE YOU
FACING YOUR CHALLENGES?

WHAT ARE YOUR CURRENT CHALLENGES?

WHAT EMOTIONS ARE YOU EXPERIENCING?

WHO IS YOUR SUPPORT?

HOW HAVE YOU GROWN?

HOW WILL YOU CONTINUE TO GROW?

Where are you Wounded?

Hurt Leaders, Hurt Leaders

Dear Leader,

The same way you form opinions of others through their actions, so will others form opinions of you. Yet, no matter how sure you are of your perspectives and opinions, know this, they are not facts. You have only used your own experiences and understanding to categorize and define what you see so that you can digest it. Nothing more, nothing less. A famous thought leader said; "Nothing has any meaning but what we give it." What meaning are you giving your presence, your worth, your work? On what is that meaning based? Who gave you the parameters by which to define it? Who defines you? Are they correct? Where did you get your definition of you?

Your first view of yourself probably comes from your parents and families. Parents facilitate your presence in this world, but they are still not the great determiners of who you are. Parents are subject to their own education, beliefs, and experiences. Unfortunately, too many parents have raised us from the space of their own pain and bitter disappointments with life. Some live vicariously through us. They have nurtured us with their anger and fears. They have taught us their lessons instead of helping us to navigate our own. It is up to you to make the choice to move past the behaviors and damaging ideas that have raised you.

It may not be easy, but it is possible. There are countless examples of successful people who by the definition of their own parents were nothing, worthless, with no value or purpose. Yet they tapped into the gifts and definition of the grand creator to prove them wrong. The only real definition of who we are is the Divine Definition. This definition supersedes all other versions of who we are perceived to be...even to ourselves.

Why would I even mention this? Because this may be one source of wounding that will affect your leadership. A wound that remains unacknowledged will remain unhealed. Unhealed wounds will become infected scars that will poison your thoughts, words, and actions. Unfortunately, this infection will not only affect you. It will, without a doubt, slowly corrupt your followers, your successors, and your legacy. This wound will have you chasing dreams and fighting shadows of demons created by your ancestors before you've ever even identified your own. This shadow boxing will distract you from uncovering the true source of your pain, and therefore inhibit your healing. You can't heal what isn't revealed.

The question becomes; "Do you desire to be healed?" If so, it will require action, honesty, and effort on your part. You are responsible for your healing. Your leadership depends on it. So many people avoid the process of healing for fear of reliving the pain of what wounded them in the first place. Avoidance does not get rid of the pain, it only prolongs it. Just because you ignore your wounds does not mean that the people looking at you don't see them. Your wounds will shut down your ability to receive feedback. Your inability and unwillingness to look at yourself and be fully aware of your wounds, blind spots, and shortcomings will render you ineffective as a leader. Without the ability to look at yourself in the mirror placed before you, you run the risk of being the toxic element in your environment. You will assume a defensive stance that will make you appear abrasive and combative. This will diminish your authority and damage your leadership legacy.

Take the time to discover the root of your wounding. Who or what hurt you? Whatever the source of your pain, you can heal from it if you so desire. Healing doesn't mean forgetting you were hurt, it means releasing what hurt you. Don't allow your unhealed pain to rob you of your chance to build your legacy.

Loss

At some point in time, YOU WILL LOSE! You have probably lost a great deal more than you imagined you would. Jobs, opportunities, money, people, relationships - different categories, but all losses. How do you hold up under the weight of loss? How do you hold up another leader under their losses?

Dear Leader,

Sometimes life knocks you down. Sometimes you will get right back up. Sometimes you will stay down and wonder if you will ever rise again. There is not an immediate fix for some situations. You may have acquired coping mechanisms and tools to help you weather these storms. However, the tools you may have are not a guarantee that you won't have pain or suffering. These tools may help you to recover quickly, but they do not exempt you from the experience of being human.

Have you spent immeasurable time and finances to evolve, educate, and enlighten yourself? The countless hours and resources that you have spent may have helped garner you a reputation as an expert or guru in your world. Your work has boosted your confidence in your ability to tackle life's challenges with a certain agility that is enviable. You've even patted yourself on the back a time or two for the manner in which you handled some tough times and people. That's great, but no matter how many times you've come through trials seemingly unbothered, there will always be those times when no amount of self-talk or self-awareness will be able to overcome the actuality of being human and having human feelings, emotions, and challenges. I've watched many leaders reach their boiling point and struggle to survive as they slowly drown in a sea of unchecked emotions.

Coming face-to-face with feelings of disappointment, doubt, confusion, fear, and even failure is an inevitable part of human existence. Maybe you feel like you are losing, even though you are winning. Or maybe your confidence falters in your abilities, even while everyone else is praising you. It looks like doubt. It looks like exhaustion and lack of motivation to go on. It looks like "Why am I doing this anyway?" Any of these insecurities can seemingly appear out of the blue. You just wake up one day and for no reason, everything feels off and nothing seems to be right! You know a pep talk isn't going to get it and you don't want to hear one. This can last for a day, for weeks, months, or longer. Though these feelings may be unfounded and irrational, the emotional and mental toll they take is real.

There may be people around you who speak what they believe to be encouraging words; "*Pray. Suck it up! No time to rest, keep going! There is nothing for you to fear. You are a champion. You are stronger than this!*" While the intention behind these encouraging words may be to help, I find that they can often have the opposite effect.

Most cultures and communities have shown themselves uncomfortable with vulnerability and anything perceived as weakness. We're so enamored with overcoming that we believe strength means never feeling anything or letting anyone know what we really feel. This ideology has been detrimental to our growth and evolution as a society. We have substituted genuine concern and care for averted eyes and tissues passed to dry the tears we don't care to see. We offer one-size-fits-all responses hoping to rush past another's discomfort in order to avoid our own. We arrogantly assume we know the answer without listening to the problem. This inadvertently says that feelings are not valid and we are uninterested in addressing the underlying issues that caused these feelings.

If I can do one thing in this letter, it would be to move you to think deeply about your actions and words and don't simply offer automated phrases of faux comfort. Real compassion requires interest in real issues.

- When is the last time someone made a statement of disappointment sadness or discouragement and you gave them space to actually share what was wrong? Did you acknowledge their fears and feelings? Did you give them a safe space to share the actual problem before you started smothering them with superficial condolences and empowering speeches? Think about the number of times you felt less-than-stellar and just wished for a safe space to be heard and not necessarily for someone to try to solve the problem. A space where you are understood, your feelings are valid, and you are allowed to be vulnerable without judgment is priceless. When is the last time you were this space for someone else?

When the Territory Scares You

Dear Leader,

You are an amazing visionary and powerful manifestor. The breakthroughs and successes you have had personally and those breakthroughs you've helped facilitate in the lives of others is evidence of your gift and grace. You make things happen. You get things done! You've learned how to tap into your intuition and how to listen to the small still voice that leads you. Your life is more than one moment of faith, it is a well-documented masterpiece of trust and surrender. You have grown by leaps and bounds by being willing to humble yourself and stretch beyond your personal capabilities to be a conduit of change. Your legacy is evident in the lives of those you have served. You have overcome so much in your lifetime, you may feel like you don't want to take on any more. Yet, you were given a vision - a vision that is deeper in-depth and greater in reach than you've ever imagined; a vision that scares you. A vision so vast that even the thought of starting, let alone where to start is overwhelming your circuits and threatening to shut you down.

So rather than moving in the direction of the vision, you seek comfort in your prior successes. You seek out the familiar feeling that being in control of the outcome gives you. I get it. You have had such high highs and such low lows just to make it to this space in time. You've paid dues that you don't feel you owed; yet, you returned to the front-lines again and again in acts of obedience to your assignment, goal, and purpose. Yet, this one is different.

The massive nature of this mission is like nothing you've ever faced before and you have serious doubts about your ability to accomplish it. This task will require more faith than you think you have, more energy than you can muster, more collaboration and trust than you think is possible. This may call for humility and patience that you might not yet possess. It may require you to share your spotlight. It might just ask you to put down the ideas about processes and timelines that you have established as a means of validation for yourself and others. You may have to release the comforts you know in order for you to touch the prize you were promised for daring to go forward without the complete picture, direction, or know-how. Faith.

This vision is calling you higher and you're afraid to answer the call. You're afraid to face or answer the question of who you will be outside of what you have been known for. Apart from the accessories that come with you. What if the identity you've been leaning on isn't it. What if there's more. What if you had to let go of all the validation you've received from external sources in order to touch the brass ring that you never even knew was possible. Is it your fear or ego guiding you? It should be your purpose.

This is a choice that only you can make. This is an answer only you can give. Can you, will you go further? Will you take the chance offered to you or will you remain safe with what you feel you already know. Will your fear send you into retreat, or will you allow faith in yourself and your source to help you to move mountains? You are capable. To help you process this decision, I have only three suggestions:

1. Halt in your tracks and ground yourself in purpose. What is your assignment here? Ground yourself in gratitude and acknowledge all you've accomplished no matter how small.

2. Recall your journey and the challenges and trials you've overcome to get to where you are - not as a source of pain but of victory and a reminder that you have overcome against all odds and impossibilities.

3. Surrender your idea/belief of what can or should look like and trust the process - walk in faith.

I don't have any witty or inspirational talks about runners and races or trials and victories to share with you. You've probably heard most of them anyway. You already know what it takes to be successful, you've just hit a wall. A wall built up by the challenge that has called into question who you are and what you can do. The one thing I do know and can share with you is your greatest chance at persevering and conquering this trial is to focus on the prize and the purpose, not the mountain you have to climb to reach it. The choice is always yours. The walk is yours alone - though you don't walk alone.

You may have to let go of the people, structures, and ideologies that you have carried with you as props and shields to protect you. It will be ok. Listen to the director.

Superheroes In Tattered Capes

Dear Leader,

People's perceptions and expectations of you will always surpass and be out of alignment with your actual capacity. As a leader, all eyes are on you. Every word you speak, every move you make is under scrutiny. They are watching to see if what you say and what you do match. Inquiring minds and prying eyes will always be paying attention, searching for your faults in order to pounce on your weaknesses. In one way this can be a great motivator to keep you accountable and responsible for the tasks, goals, and promises you have laid out for those you will lead. On the other hand, it can also become a trap of isolation, fear, and false appearances that you will strain to maintain at the cost of your true identity and sanity.

No matter what your intentions or your track record, people's perceptions of you will always be based on their personal emotions and experiences. Even though people have the right to hold their leaders to a higher standard in regards to ethics, integrity, and accountability - this belief or expectation usually overrides and ignores the reality of real-life; in real-time, being experienced by a leader. In a society where superheroes equal saviors and are who we

97

believe will right all the wrongs and fix all the problems we could encounter, we don't often look deeply at the personal conflicts and complicated aspects of life for them. We don't get an insider look at those moments when it all becomes too much to handle, and the normal superhuman response doesn't come easily or maybe not at all.

In old comics and movies, the conflict is often glossed over and romanticized for us to root and cheer for their return to saving and being saviors. We consume and enjoy their storyline all the while knowing in our hearts (and because of cinematic effects) that they will overcome the challenge. We know they will fight through the moment of weakness and return to their duty of saving the world as if this were only a minor insignificant blip on the radar of their lives. We have been so trained that trouble only lasts for a short while that we translate this unrealistic expectation of instant healing to our real-life leaders - believing they will always respond like superheroes do in the movies.

We believe that they will always opt to do what is for our greatest good, for the cause, or for anybody else that they serve. Therefore making leadership an unsafe space in which to dwell. We abuse our leadership and we abuse ourselves as leaders when we succumb to the ideology that we are not allowed to be human in our emotions or responses to life and its many challenges. Leaders are told to cry in the dark and hide our trauma, disappointment, and pain. We are told it's not okay to not be okay. We are taught that showing our flaws, uncertainties, mistakes, and fears is a sign of weakness and therefore calls into question our abilities as a leader. What is woefully missing from this equation is instruction on how to face and navigate through these situations.

I must admit, I love a good hero story as much as anyone, and I too have been guilty of expecting a quick bounce back and perfect recovery from people I viewed as leaders, myself included. I have oftentimes been my own harshest critic. Have you done that too? Have you been oblivious to the emotions and challenges that could be affecting you? Your leaders? Have you chosen to ignore humanity? At what cost?

I have found that I actually like to see a hero's flaws. For me, it makes them more relatable and believable. Every hero/leader has a behind the scenes challenge, and sometimes it's a war. Look at these Superheroes and see if you see yourself or the leaders you know in them.

Think of **Superman** fighting with his identity in the form of Clark Kent. He fiercely fought to fit in as a *nor-*

mal guy. Hiding his gift from the world, afraid of being exposed for his differences. He endured being overlooked and underestimated by people who had no clue of his true capabilities or purpose. People who spoke ill of him degraded him and described him as useless. (Identity Crisis)

Spider Man suffered from guilt and a lack of self-worth. Feeling responsible for the loss of and the inability to be the savior of the people he cared about. Full of guilt and shame for his perceived failure. So he kept saving people who wanted his solutions but didn't want him. (Savior Syndrome)

Wonder Woman, seemingly impervious to anything thrown her way and always seeking truth, finally reached a breaking point when the foundation of her beliefs and ideas of herself was broken by an unknown truth. Her identity and life work were completely disrupted causing her to question who she was. (Nervous Breakdown - Trauma)

Batman was traumatized at an early age and lost his ability to trust people or the systems of justice that were in place. This led him to only trust himself and operate in isolation, with no long term partnerships. He operated with the constant need to have complete control over every aspect of his existence. This challenge was exacerbated by the fact that no matter how much good he did, most of those who benefitted from his help did not appreciate him and actually thought he was a menace. (Control Issues)

Does any of this sound familiar or relatable? While their hero personas tend to loom larger than life and defy logic, time, space, and circumstance, their personal struggles are no less trying for them than they are for us mere mortals. Their gifts and strengths seemingly allow them to bear the burdens of the world in their hands, yet unable to overcome their own inner demons. They contend with the blocks of their own; "How do you do it"? Their struggles require them to dig from a deeper well in order to tap into a strength to fight what their gifts and superpowers are powerless against. What do they do when what they stand for and their response to particular circumstances do not line up?

Like our superheroes, we as leaders often contribute to others at great personal cost. Loss of family and friends, rejection, abandonment, and betrayal. We struggle with why we do what we do, if this really is our purpose, being rejected and villainized, being unappreciated, and loneliness. We wonder if we are crazy for continuing. We wonder if we can continue. We face people who intentionally seek to destroy us. We bear self-inflicted traumas of guilt and shame. So many of us are operating at a fraction of our ability and doing the best we can from a fractured psyche. We are equal parts hero and villain - the viewpoint depending on the viewer.

Understand that you are not alone. You are never always the hero nor the villain, and even Superheroes have to check out at some point in order to mend their tattered capes.

Leading While Bleeding

Dear Leader,

Sometimes, in spite of your best efforts and intentions, your results will fall flat or fail miserably. No one wins all the time - not our superheroes, not our super leaders, not you. Even our fictional leaders were plagued with the emotional and mental aftermath of seemingly meaningless efforts to make a difference and failed attempts to save the world. Many of our heroes fictional and non-fictional have suffered bouts of depression as a result of these on-going battles with the call of duty versus the reality of personal challenges.

Leaders like Martin Luther King Jr., Abraham Lincoln, Gandhi, and Princess Diana all fell into depression at some point in their journeys. Some even battled with suicidal tendencies! Yet the world didn't care to hear or relay that part of their existence. Depression, anxiety, anger, or the challenges of life in general just don't make a good 'hero' story. So these very real, very human parts become taboo and are generally left out of the narrative. Thus creating the illusion of shiny, happy, and perfect leaders who are in fact leading while bleeding.

You were taught that leaders don't make excuses, and you shouldn't. However, being transparent about your shortcomings while in the midst of your trials has erroneously been categorized as 'making excuses'. Because of this, you tend to keep your trials to yourself for fear of judgment and add the weight of fear of failure and disappointing others onto your already heavy load as a leader. You may become consumed with guilt when things don't go as planned or when you are unable to please everyone. Then you act as if what you are experiencing is not a viable reason for your less than stellar performance. I am not a mental health expert, but I know that this is not a healthy or sustainable mindset. It is not odd to feel discouraged when faced with the despair and inequities in this world. Knowing that you have an important part in the transformation can feel like you are constantly battling a hydra, the multi-headed monster of Greek mythology, cut off one head and three more grow. Never-ending. Exhausting.

I recently experienced first-hand the unexpected valley of depression that blew into my life after a series of disappointments, dead-ends, and actual death. All of which occurred within a matter of months in rapid succession -

no breaks, no recovery time. This came after years of hard work and seeming to overcome major trials, losses, and setbacks. At the end of 2019, all of these issues came to a head and I had reached my breaking point; for the second time in 2 years. I was ready to leave my superhero cape behind and walk away from it all. I was drowning in disappointment, discouragement, and loss. I couldn't breathe. I was emotionally, physically, and spiritually exhausted. I hated the very idea of helping anyone else. Something in me had broken and I knew that I needed to heal before I reached the point of no return. My cape was tattered and full of holes. So what did I do? I stepped back from everything. I put on my oxygen mask in order to save myself. I chose me. I told as many people as I could, those that I worked with and those seeking me for guidance that I was not okay and I was taking a break in order to preserve myself and my work. Funny enough, me choosing me didn't go over well with a lot of people. Everyone didn't understand what I was doing, but it was a risk that I was willing to take. That I needed to take.

I share this insight with you, not for sympathy, but to let you know that none of us are exempt. This happened to me two times within a 4 year period! No class or mantra will exclude you from this part of leadership. I had every type of healing tool and methodology at my disposal to assist me in navigating this minefield of emotion, yet they could not prevent me from actually going through the process of feeling the pain to be able to heal the pain. Even as I write to you now, know that I am in the final stages of recovery that allow me to share this most important guidance with you.

My experience reminds me of the false idea in leadership that martyrdom is an admirable goal. Too often leaders are expected to be willing to irrationally sacrifice themselves without hesitation for the greater good - whatever or whomever that may be at the time. Martyrdom has been so romanticized that we've been led to believe that to *not* sacrifice ourselves is selfish. While there may definitely be a need for self-sacrifice at times, not every instance requires that type of offering from us, and you as a wise leader will do well to use discernment in making that decision.

No matter how passionate or convicted we are to a cause or an idea, we as individuals are a limited commodity and therefore limited in the energy that we have to expend. Choose wisely. When you choose to run continuously without refueling your mind, body, and spirit, you hinder one of the most powerful tools to your success, your intuition and divine connection. You can live to fight another battle by being willing to cut losses and pull back in order to regroup and move forward with renewed strength, and a refreshed mind and spirit. In our western philosophy taking a break is usually interpreted as the end...someone else is coming to take your place. This is a lie set in a lack mentality. What is for you is for you. The spotlight of leadership will challenge this idea at every turn.

Being in the eye of the public under constant scrutiny is not an easy chair to sit in. Being criticized, praised, loved, and hated by a bi-polar public and an ever-changing tide of cancel culture sparked by whatever opinion is popular with the public at the moment can understandably lead to self-doubt, self-depreciation, and condemnation, none of which is healthy for self-esteem.

Some of us have survived horrific things publicly or privately, known and unknown. It's a wonder that we're still holding on by whatever thin life-line that keeps us here. Many of us battle daily with the fear of being found out. "*If the world knew the truth about who I am, what I've done or what's been done to me, then surely I will be reject-ed."* These fears tend to be the foundation of the argument for why we must keep all of our trials and weaknesses hidden and build the facade of impenetrability and perfection. Admit no wrongs, show no vulnerability. The wall of protection we believe we are building to insulate ourselves from pain, slowly transforms into the prison that restricts our growth and prevents our access to a life of freedom. A prison that eventually destroys our identity.

In our efforts to suppress our painful truths and traumas, we can in actuality create a catalyst for greater harm to ourselves and others around us. We become so consumed with hiding our private selves from everyone else that we don't notice when we actually begin to believe our public lie and lose our true identity. Though these are valid concerns and feelings, if we do not address them, they can overwhelm us and become a factor in derailing our progress and legacy.

There may come a time when it all becomes too much for you to bear and you'll want out, but there may be no exit or relief in sight. The odds may seem stacked against you and no help is evident. People may check on you or check out when you no longer fulfill the roles they have set for you in their lives. They may fade away because they don't know what to do when their vision of the *strong you* is overshadowed by your present state of vulnerability. Some simply won't care. This is the time for you to choose yourself. Self-preservation can be self-care.

Some people will not agree with what I am about to tell you, and that's ok. Old habits die hard and hero syndrome is real. However, this may prove to be a key to your longevity and survival as a leader. TAKE A BREAK! It may seem unfathomable to pause or step away. It may be impossible to see the light from where you are. This is the time to have enough faith in your value and purpose to take your moment. Pause, scream, cry, mourn, meditate, sleep, pray. Whatever your pause looks like, take it! As uncomfortable or irresponsible as it may seem to others and yourself, it is necessary. Even God took a rest from His work. Rest is necessary for our healing and recovery. If being in a pandemic taught us anything, we learned that everything does better with a bit of downtime.

Our resiliency is directly linked to our regeneration processes. You may not be in a space to be able to take an extended time away, however, you can build time for yourself into each day at best; each week at the least. No matter what your job, business, family culture says, it is not meant for you to give every part of yourself away 24 hours a day. Week after week. Month after month. Year after year. Take this time to make an honest assessment of where you are, what you are feeling, and how it is affecting you. You may try to avoid taking this deep honest look because you're afraid of what you might find, the pain it may cause and the decisions you may have to make as a result. But I promise it will be worth it, and with practice, it will become a life-altering ritual.

Dear Leader

MEND YOUR CAPE

WHAT PART OF YOU NEEDS ATTENTION?

WHAT IS RECEIVING YOUR ENERGY?

WHERE IS YOUR SAFE SPACE?

WHAT IS YOUR TRUTH AT THIS MOMENT?

HOW WILL YOU CREATE SPACE TO REST AND RECOVER FROM LEADING?

Failure and Falling

"Failure should be our teacher, not our undertaker. Failure is delay, not defeat. It is a temporary detour, not a dead end. Failure is something we can avoid only by saying nothing, doing nothing, and being nothing."

- Denis Waitley

Dear Leader,

You were chosen and you agreed to serve. Yet, somewhere along the way, what that means has been lost. The people (whoever they are) as a whole have put their confidence and hope in you. Hope that you will also choose them in return. That you will be fair and impartial, that you will keep your word and fulfill your promises. Yet, here we are, and this looks nothing like what you expected. Somewhere along the way, you kept making "left turns" and now you seem to have forgotten how to make a right one.

It's not too late to recover from your mistake, but a herculean effort is required, and you will have to humble yourself to ask for mercy and grace that maybe you yourself have not shown to others. You will need to admit you were wrong and accept the consequences of your actions. That in itself can prove to be more challenging than taking any other action. I mean, who wants to be responsible for what they've said and done? Who wants to face the consequences of their actions - especially if you've escaped detection, not been held accountable, and have suffered no negative repercussions. Maybe, you have even been rewarded for your bad behavior. Ignore it and maybe it will go away. Why not simply lie, close your eyes, and pretend that you have no clue what they're talking about?

113

Why not? Because you made a promise, swore an oath, and gave your word You were chosen. It's ok to make a mistake. It is not ok to cover it up or justify why you did. You have a lot of missteps to undo and you're not sure where to start. You're going to have to start with your own house, with you. In order to begin to make amends, you need to go back to the origin of it all. Why did you become a leader? Who are you serving? What has worked, what hasn't? Where did you veer off course? When did you lose your focus on your purpose and goal, and subsequently, your honor? HOW do you get back on track?

This is not an answer, but a guideline. When your life is in turmoil and the world is upside down the best you can do for yourself is to pause and go back to your foundation. Ask yourself those discovery questions and then take actions that are rooted in integrity, even if you lost some integrity and your morals were corrupted along the way. Decide to do better and correct your mistakes. This may mean removing yourself completely from the position you are in. That may not be what you want to do, but it may be what you need to do. Not only to heal yourself but to also heal those you have wronged through your actions. Accountability isn't just about saying you were wrong, it is also about taking care of those that you have wronged, even if it means you must leave them in the care of another.

The Apology

Dear Leader,

What are you apologizing for? Is your apology sincere? Should you even apologize at all? In this day in age, it is near impossible to say or do anything without offending or upsetting at least one person or group of people. You cannot please everyone. So How and when should you apologize?

First, ask yourself what is the purpose of an apology? In recent years we've seen apologies become more frequent and less sincere. Our visibility culture has turned apologies into a series of comments made for optics or as proverbial "get out of jail" free cards. Many public apologies are at best a nice way of saying *shut up and move on*. As a result, we find it hard to believe most of the apologies that we hear. We are cynical of the motives behind the apology and wonder if it is only an act of attrition to avoid being held accountable. These are valid questions.

A funny thing, the word *apology* is by one of its definitions: a very poor or inadequate example of something. This definition seems to have overtaken the primary meaning, which according to the Oxford dictionary is: a regretful acknowledgment of an offense or failure. So which definition fits your idea of what an apology is?

I'll share with you mine. I believe a true apology is not just an acknowledgment of an offense or failure, but it is a form of revelation. A revelation of a blindspot or misstep that a person may not have recognized before. I would like to believe that most offenses are committed from a space of true ignorance or oversight, but I know that many are committed with intention and disregard for consequences. As my mother would say; "They're not sorry, they're just sorry they got caught!"

How then do you gauge the authenticity of an apology? For me, a heartfelt apology is accompanied by a change in behavior; not just the words, "I'm sorry". Apology is a sign of repentance. Without action, there is no repentance. An apology without changed behavior is manipulation. If an apology is offered simply to avoid consequences, it is a lie.

A quick side note about receiving or not receiving an apology. There is a standard that many of us hold regarding receiving an apology. Regardless of whether or not an apology meets your approval, do not allow yourself to be in bondage because of it. Bondage? We can unwittingly create a prison for ourselves and others based on the idea of receiving an apology we feel we deserve. How so? By making the decision to continue to hold on to an offense and use it as the basis for our anger and indignation. We refuse to move past the transgression and instead operate as the "offended party" that is owed restitution. Restitution that is only deemed acceptable if it is received when we want it, the way that we want it. In this manner, we allow our pride to commandeer our emotions and actions, becoming puffed up and entitled. The longer we hold on, the worse it becomes. Before we know it, we are spreading our poisoned perceptions to others and seeking allies to join us in our quest to be acknowledged as a victim of wrongdoing. This behavior is the seed that can lead to feuds and division amongst leaders and members of businesses, organizations, and families. This is the seed that blossoms into the weed of bitterness and unforgiveness. Unforgiveness, in turn, contaminates not only our countenance but more importantly, our spirit. This has the ability to single-handedly destroy the value of any perceived good we may do by affecting our heart condition. If there is unforgiveness residing in our hearts, it will inhibit our ability to attain the peace, joy, and blessings we seek.

With that being said, I am not an apologist. I do not necessarily like to apologize, so I try to be mindful of the things that I say and do so that I am able to stand in integrity behind my actions. Does that mean I never apologize? No, it simply means that when I do, it *is* sincere because I am experiencing a revelation and not seeking to escape the consequences of something I intentionally did.

I believe apologies should also be in season. I don't believe in apologizing forever. It serves no purpose but to be a never-ending reminder that a mistake was made. As an offense is committed and called to our attention, we should seek to make amends. However, I do not believe in continually being reminded of the offense and expected to be contrite anytime it is bought up. This is not forgiveness - of self or others. Continually holding a person's offense over their head keeps both parties in bondage. It supports the false narrative that a person is their mistakes and holds them hostage to those mistakes. This blocks growth. While some transgressions can be deemed worse than others, the spirit of guilt, shame, and victimhood attached to constant apology is burdensome and does not provide relief. We must learn to release others and ourselves from this burden.

By learning to mitigate your expectations and avoid imposing them on others, you will liberate yourself in so many ways. You will no longer be bound by unmet expectations, trespasses, or the disappointment of insincere apologies or even the apologies you may not ever receive. Lastly, being offended is always a choice. If you choose to hold onto offense and make it your crutch to help you limp along in victimhood, then you will reside in a prison of your own making.

Recovery

After you have gone through the fire, made
your mistakes, fallen down and cried your tears
...Course-correct and GET BACK UP!

Your Leadership

Dear Leader,

What type of leader are you here to be? Are you a leader-of-leaders, or a leader-of-followers? Are you called to be a voice to the masses, delivering inspiration and hope to those looking for direction, or are you called to be the voice of wisdom to those destined to lead and in need of mentoring, guidance, support, and encouragement? Do you know? Why should you know? Determining who your intended audience is will not only help shape the message you deliver, it will also help you to get clear about who you are actually serving. Determining *who* you are called to lead will help you to understand *how* best to lead them. This type of clarity will save you the wasted time and frustration of chasing people and seeking validation from those you were not meant for in the first place. Everything is not for everybody. Neither are you and your message for everyone. Knowing who you serve will enable you to eliminate unnecessary tactics and ploys to try to draw people to you that you are not assigned to.

Are you a leader-of-leaders, or a leader-of-followers? As I continue to train and support leaders, this is one of the first questions I ask them. An overwhelming majority of them do not respond immediately because they have in fact never taken time to think about it, and thus do not know. That is the epitome of leading blindly. If you do not know who you are as a leader, you will not know who you are to serve, and this makes you vulnerable to corrupting your message to please everyone! When you are willing to pander to be popular, your integrity is compromised, your impact as a leader is weakened, and confidence in your abilities will die. We've all seen this in action in our workplace, in our churches, in our governments. Those leaders who never seem to take a firm stand on any issues for fear of losing favor and popularity. Those leaders that solely follow the advice of advisors with agendas because they lack the confidence in themselves to have an agenda of their own. Or the leader who bullies because they believe *everyone* should follow them and that they are entitled to their admiration and allegiance simply because of their position. These are the types of leaders that lack self-awareness, integrity, and clear purpose.

How do you know what type of leader you are? Before you can get to who you are leading, there are some things about yourself you should review. Do you have an affinity for smaller groups of people or large crowds? Are you like a rockstar with that certain charisma that attracts people like moths to a flame? Do people seek you out for advice, counsel, and direction? Paying attention to all of these things will give you clues as to what type of leader you are and who you are here to serve. Leadership is service first.

For the sake of ease and clarity, I would like to give the simplest description of these two leadership styles:

- **A leader-of-followers (lof)** is generally a leader with charisma and the ability to draw and move a crowd. They do well being in front of crowds. Their followers like the way they make them feel. They tend to have the ability to easily influence people and garner attention for whatever they do. They have the ability to reach large general groups of people. People like to be in their presence and *follow* their words, actions, and deeds. They *tell* people what to do.

- **A leader-of-leaders (lol)** tends to serve in a more advisory capacity. They may be visible but often are behind the scenes. They may or may not do well in front of a crowd. They tend to function well in smaller circles and on smaller platforms. Their followers like what they teach and seek them out for wisdom and counsel, how they make them feel is secondary. This leader seeks to empower and prepare their followers to lead others. Their followers are **leaders**. They **teach** people what to do.

These definitions are general and by no means absolute in terms of explanation. However, they are a good start for the person who has never known there is a difference. The characteristics vary from person to person and can cross over. With this basic guideline, you should be able to at least start to define what type of leader you are. It will also help you to identify the types of leaders around you. So is one better than the other or more important? The short and long answer is 'No'. Both types of leaders are important, and both have their place. I feel that these two types of leadership work well with each other and create a balance. How so? Bear with me, please.

You may have heard the very true term, "Every coach needs a coach". People in leadership positions usually have had someone to mentor them and guide them in making decisions that led them to leadership. The smart leader will always have someone who is capable of speaking into their lives and providing wise counsel to help them navigate their leadership position. They have a someone or someone's who can see their blind spots and help them to maneuver the obstacle course of leadership. Leaders need leadership. When a person is leading the crowd (lof), they need the kind of support that a follower cannot provide, and this is what a leader-of-leaders provides. They speak into the life and purpose of those leading the crowd while keeping them integral and accountable. Meanwhile, by serving the leader-of-followers, the leader-of-leaders is fulfilling their duty to teach and prepare the leader as well as promoting sound decision making that will affect the lives of those under the care of the leader. When properly aligned, It all works together for the good of all involved.

I discovered early on that I am a leader-of-leaders. I thrive in the background as a wise counsel to those in the forefront. You may not know me, but you may know my words. I may not have a million followers, but I impact millions. How? Because I impact the one who speaks to millions. Does this mean that I can't come to the forefront? No. It simply means that when I emerge, I know my position and my power, therefore, I do not struggle while I am there. That is the influence of a leader-of-leaders.

If you are unclear who you serve, it will be even less clear how you are to serve them. If you want to amplify your abilities and lead powerfully, please take the time to learn who you are as a leader so as to understand who you lead.

Your Inner Circle

Dear Leader,

You will need help to lead. No matter how smart, strong, powerful, or accomplished you are, you cannot do it alone. You will need eyes to see what you do not. You will need ears to hear what you cannot. You will need the wisdom that comes from experiences that are not your own. You will need accountability. You will need correction. You will need honest feedback. You will need loyal support. You will need hands to hold. You will need shoulders to cry on. You will need shelter from the storms. You will need those that watch your back and those that can see ahead. You will need all of these people to not only mature you as a leader, but to protect you as well. How do you find them?

That will depend greatly on you. First, you must be willing to receive what each of these persons has to offer your life and leadership. You cannot benefit from what you aren't willing to take in. Some of us lack the discipline, patience, and humility it takes to receive guidance. We choose to barrel forward in an effort to be self-made. We pridefully decline feedback and assistance so that no one can say we owe them anything. All the while struggling unnecessarily. Making it hard on ourselves. Be open to receive.

Second, you need to be discerning about who is around you, their motives, and intentions. You also need to be honest about your own motives and intentions. Many leaders are surrounded by 'yes' men who are so enamored by them that they will *never* speak truthfully or wisely for fear of losing access to them. These leaders seek guidance from unwise and inexperienced sources in order to feel powerful and have their egos stroked. They surround themselves with minions in an effort to mask their own insecurities and inadequacies instead of healing and growing. They are so enthralled with their own presence that they often miss the true agenda of these minions. They may be there to undermine or misguide. Some simply want access to power. People love access. Who has access to you? If a leader chooses not to be intentional about who has access to them they risk exposing themselves to exploitation.

Third, you need to be self-aware and willing to receive feedback. Feedback is not about judgment, it is about how you show up and how others experience you. This is tricky for many of us because feedback sounds like a fancy way of saying criticism. It is not. While there will be people who will enjoy nothing better than to tell you all the ways you are failing and inadequate, feedback is not that. Feedback is a way for a person to share with you how you 'show-up' in the world. We all have blind spots about our behaviors and how we think we appear to outside observers. Feedback helps to remove the mask. Feedback is revelatory, not accusatory. But it may still hurt nonetheless. When you are mature enough to receive it, it will transform you as a leader. Don't miss the feedback.

Fourth, *when the student is ready, the teacher appears.* When you are ready, they will show up. As you work on yourself, seek knowledge, and trust the process, you will attract who you need when you need them. Be on the lookout. Some may come for a season and some may stay for a lifetime. Whatever the case may be, remember to be grateful for the gifts they bring and the lessons that they teach. Choose wisely, choose wisdom.

Your Voice

Dear Leader,

Where is your voice? Are you able to speak or are you imprisoned in fear that keeps you silent? We live in a world where controversy or the next big protest is only a social media post or leaked recording away from occurring. It seems as if a new movement is born daily. We have become a world of conclusion jumpers that become fixated on uncorroborated pieces of our own interpretations. This makes it perilous to speak without clear interpretations and scary for some to speak at all. Who wants to be misquoted or misrepresented? No one. So many have opted to remain quiet to avoid stirring the pot and becoming the center of controversy. Many leaders opt to speak in politically correct statements and neutral noncommittal phrases to avoid sparking more controversy or appearing to favor one side over another. Thereby not standing for anything. They are too concerned with appearances or losing followers and their support, so they remain silent.

While you shouldn't speak or act on every issue you see, you have been given a voice for a reason. Have you decided what subject is worthy of, or requiring your voice? Are you so concerned with protecting your image or brand that you are willing to be silent to injustice? Are you too afraid to stand? A leader is not required to have a public opinion on every public matter, and a wise leader will use wisdom and discernment before lending their voice to an issue. But what about those high visibility, sensitive and unpopular topics like racism, sexism, criminal activities, discrimination, religion, etc.? There is a never-ending list of volatile subjects that we might want to avoid, but there comes a time when each of us must choose to speak out. The Pandemic exposed many so-called leaders through their silence. We have heard the voices of the common people like never before. The glaring disparities in health, wealth, and access has caused normally silent people to raise their voices and speak out against injustice. Where are you?

This is not meant to judge your contribution, shame you, or force you into contribution. This is meant as a point of introspection and personal evaluation. Are you using the voice you have been given for the purpose you have been assigned? Are you speaking up for others; for yourself? What is the message you are conveying with your voice? What are you waiting for?

Speaking up may cause you to lose friends, supporters, and likes. How do you decide if it's worth it? Let truth, compassion, and love for humanity to be your guide and motivator. I wish I could say that would be enough and that you'll always win and be rewarded for this. I can't... and you won't. There will be times when you are the only one on your side sharing an unpopular opinion. I believe it is better to lose everything for speaking the truth and standing for what's just rather than to silently blend into the background cowering from sight. Sometimes it is difficult to determine which side of an argument/issue one should stand on. Sometimes you will be on the winning team. Sometimes you won't. Choose your battles, and have peace with those choices. Let love, compassion, integrity, and truth guide you. Notice I didn't use right or wrong as guidelines. Right and wrong are divisive and are subject to popularity, laws, cultural norms, etc. My favorite example of this is slavery. At one time it was legal. *Everything moral is not legal, and everything legal is not moral.* Don't strive to be right, strive to be humane, honest, virtuous, and loving.

You may feel like you don't have a voice or that it has been stolen from you. You may feel like you have nothing to say or that what you have to say is unimportant. Nothing is further from the truth! Your voice is an expression of your gifts. Your voice is transformational. Your voice is healing. Your voice is necessary. Your voice is powerful! Sing with it. Scream with it. Teach with it. Heal with it. Speak with it. The world needs to hear it!

On compassion

Dear Leader,

Nobody Cares! Do You? Has constant scrutiny, judgment, and perfectionism caused you to lose your humanity and compassion? Where exactly did you learn compassion? Did you ever learn it? Have you ever been shown these qualities to actually know what they are and what they look like? Has your view of compassion been shaped by a strong moral vision or are you mimicking fragmented views put in place by your environment? Are you willing to create a different or new and improved version of what you've been shown?

Compassion is the act of being moved by sympathy to alleviate the pain of another. In other words, not just *feeling* sorry for someone's suffering, but taking action to mitigate their pain. The need for compassion is greater now more than ever. The whole world is suffering under the weight of the pain and loss stemming from the Pandemic. Loss of livelihood, loss of health, loss of community, loss of life. Before the Pandemic, we seemed to have lost the realization of our need for community and each other for our survival. Somewhere along the way, it became every man for himself, and the belief that we do this alone was introduced. The idea that we could live together in harmony and coexist in peace became suppressed distant ideas. The Pandemic showed us differently. We began to mourn the loss of what we had taken for granted. Collectively we underwent the pain of isolation, fear, and uncertainty. We needed and expected compassion; not just for others but also for ourselves. Compassion had a rebirth.

Understand that people's fears and pain manifest in different ways. It can appear as anger, indifference, stress, depression, violence and so much more. We may find it hard to express compassion for someone else while we are in the midst of feeling the need for compassion ourselves. That is reality; yet, I implore you as a leader to stretch yourself to respond with kindness first. If you can't be kind, strive to be understanding. The more you seek to understand before you respond, the greater the likelihood is that you will show compassion. Compassion must start somewhere. Let it start with you.

On humanity

In the midst of the world being turned upside down, we were forced to learn lessons of humanity. Spaces were created to respect diversity and differences. We began to celebrate and respect the ideas, creations, perspectives, and experiences of others. Though the media would try to tell us differently. There was good news. Some of us may not have reached the level of awareness that recognizes all humanity, but it's coming. In order to see the humanity in others, we must recognize and accept our own. Judge not lest ye be judged. Be willing to put ourselves in someone else's shoes. We must seek to understand as we desire to be understood. We must learn to forgive others as we want to receive forgiveness. We must make room to love others as we love ourselves.

Your Legacy

"Your life has a timeline, but your legacy doesn't."

— Lisa Nichols

Dear Leader,

The best and brightest leaders don't just shine because of what they do, they shine because of who they impact. The greatest leaders understand that what makes them truly powerful is their ability to impart knowledge and build up other leaders. They replicate themselves. Replication does not mean making minions and followers who act like them, walk like them, and talk like them. I'm speaking of replication in terms of them identifying leaders, acknowledging their gifts, giving them guidance on how to amplify their talents, encouraging them to share their gifts, and then pay it forward. Wash, rinse, repeat. This is how legacy is built.

There was a time when a community's survival was based on shared knowledge. Ensuring that as many people as possible had vital information as it pertained to safety and survival was the mark of a good leader. Fathers took pride in passing down their knowledge to their sons, and mothers built whole societies around sharing the secrets of healing and life with their daughters. The custom of passing down knowledge not only preserved traditions and history, but it played a key part in laying a strong foundational identity for generations to be established upon. As this practice waned and information was shared amongst fewer people, thirst for power took over. Knowledge is power, and sadly in an effort to maintain sole power and importance, people with access to knowledge, have limited the flow of information.

As a leader, it is fundamental that you unblock the dam and share what you know with those around you. Never allow the fear of being outshone to make you lose sight of who you are and your duty as a leader. As a reminder, that duty is to share your gifts and talents with the world in order to inspire and guide others to do the same. You have a special responsibility to those that have been entrusted to you. You are to behave as wise counsel to mentor and prepare them for the eventuality of their leadership role. I feel that when we do not properly nurture those that we have been given to care for, we are robbing God. As leaders, we should be setting an example worth following. We should be creating a culture of contribution in which this is a standard. Those we lead should receive this as part of their inheritance from our tutelage.

One of my favorite examples of the replication I am speaking of is the United States Army Special Forces, better known as The Green Berets. The Green Berets have garnered respect as one of the most elite and deadly military forces in the world. While most people believe that the Green Berets are deadly because of their ability to infiltrate and kill, that is not what makes them so lethal. They are the deadliest because of their ability to train and replicate themselves. Though they operate in only twelve-man teams, their strength comes from their ability to train and lead. I read once that one of these teams can enter a country with little to no military presence and raise and train a sizable army of guerilla fighters within only 30 days.

Green Berets are elite because they operate in the spirit of excellence and therefore only accept those believed to be the best of the best. This is their core group of leaders, their strong inner circle. They learn to trust and operate as a unit. They are extensively trained and prepared before they are even considered to be put in position. Though they operate as one, they are not carbon copies of each other. They don't believe in everybody being the same. They recognize and utilize the unique talents of each soldier in their unit. Each member of their twelve-man team is a specialist in a specific area. They understand that each person has a purpose and they support them in carrying out their duties. They then teach what they know, and teach others to do the same. This makes them force multipliers. This is my idea model of what powerful leadership and the building of powerful leaders look like. What is your method for replicating yourself and building up the next generation of leaders? What legacy are you building? This will be a part of your legacy.

Dear Leader,

I see you. I am a witness to your trials and your triumphs. I am cheering you on and praying for your success. I believe that you have what it takes to make the difference and you will. As you continue to elevate and evolve, may you always remain firmly grounded in WHO you are and WHOSE you are. You are the direct result of a divine vision. You were designed to be the answer to someone's prayer. It may be difficult to believe that at times, but it's true.

As you think and believe, so will you see. Monitor your thoughts and take care of your mind. Your mind is powerful and the home of your dreams and visions.

Listen more than you speak. Practice hearing for understanding, not to respond. Hear with your heart and spirit. Learn to protect what you receive through your ears, so as not to contaminate your mind and your heart. May what you hear bring you balance and comfort.

You are a visionary. There may be times when your vision gets cloudy and you feel like you are stumbling blindly through life. You may feel like you have lost your sight and your way. In these times it is important to know from where the vision originated. When you are clear about who gave you the assignment, you are less likely to deviate from it. Keep your eyes on the prize. Remember you are the product of the Master Visionary.

You create worlds with your words. Use your words to empower those that hear them. Your voice can create a sound that will resonate throughout the earth. In your voice lies the power to raise up nations and tear down tyrants. Your words bring to life your vision; be mindful of what you say. Use your words to speak well of yourself and those you meet. Your word can be a bond or a bind. Speak with the intention of edifying and uplifting. You have the power to curse and to bless with your mouth. Speak blessings.

Let everything you touch feel the presence of healing and love. Touch with the intention to nurture and to build. Hold with the intention to uplift. Let the evidence of your vision spring forth from your hands. Let your touch be felt beyond your reach.

Walk boldly forward with full confidence that you are an intentional creation. Step intentionally in the direction of your vision. Know that you are leaving footprints behind that others are following. Choose your path wisely. Walk in faith that you will complete the journey. Walk in faith that you are not alone.

You may look different from me, you may be from a different time, space, and culture, but we share some of the same goals; to impact the world and leave a legacy. People will question you and life will challenge you. Things may not go your way. Remember you always have a choice in how you respond, what you will take away, and what you will release. Don't forget to release.

The time has come for your gifts, voice, and creations to be released. You are creating for the next generation. You are healing for the generations past. What are you creating? How will you be remembered? What will be your legacy?

You are a Curse Breaker. You are a Blessing Activator. You are a Legacy Builder.

Dear Leader, leave your legacy! Dear Leader, you are loved!

Dear Leader

LEADERSHIP & LEGACY

WHO IS IN YOUR INNER CIRCLE?

WHAT TYPE OF LEADER ARE YOU?

DO YOU NEED TO APOLOGIZE? IF SO, TO WHOM?

HOW ARE SHARING YOUR KNOWLEDGE?

HOW ARE YOU BUILDING YOUR LEGACY AND HOW ARE YOU INCLUDING YOUR INNER CIRCLE IN YOUR LEGACY?

NOTES

NOTES

NOTES

Made in the USA
Columbia, SC
22 May 2024

35619130R00090